60 Plant-Based Treats for Any Occasion

# Fantastic Vegan Cookies

Tiina Strandberg, Creator of My Berry Forest

PAGE STREET
PUBLISHING CO.

PAGE STREET
PUBLISHING CO.

First published in 2021 by
Page Street Publishing Co.
27 Congress Street, Suite 105
Salem, MA 01970
www.pagestreetpublishing.com

Distributed by Macmillan, sales in Canada by The Canadian Manda Group.

25  24  23  22  21    1  2  3  4  5

ISBN-13: 978-1-64567-352-1
ISBN-10: 1-64567-352-9

Library of Congress Control Number: 2021931354

Cover and book design by Kylie Alexander for Page Street Publishing Co.
Photos by Tiina Strandberg

Printed and bound in China

This book is dedicated to you, my friend, a cookie lover and hopefully an enthusiastic cookie baker too. It is also dedicated to my family: my three little ones, calm husband, loving parents and the best sister and her family. This book is made possible because of your love and support.

# Table of Contents

# Introduction

Welcome, dear cookie lovers and bakers, to the world of *Fantastic Vegan Cookies*!

This baking book with 60 delicious vegan cookie recipes is made for you. I believe there's a cookie monster inside us all, just waiting for a chance to grab a cookie or two. Now is your chance to start baking the most wonderful, fantastic vegan cookies to make your cookie monster happy.

I have a cookie for you in this book for all occasions and cookie cravings, from the traditional indulgent chocolate flavors and fruity and berry-filled jam cookies to scrumptious cookie bars featuring both twists on classics and new, exciting flavors. I am delighted to share a variety of my favorite cookie recipes and amazing Nordic flavors in this book too.

I have also included a good selection of wholesome snack cookies for you, featuring cookies with nuts, seeds, dates and berries and even a few savory cookies to enjoy as part of your snack platter or vegan cheese board. The last chapter of the book is full of easy-to-make no-bake treats with both healthier versions of classic treats and totally decadent gooey caramel treats covered in chocolate.

Fantastic vegan cookies come in all shapes, sizes and colors, but they have more in common than their deliciousness: They are all rustic and cozy. With this book I want to show you how easy and fun vegan cookie baking is—no fancy techniques, ingredients or decorations are required. The results are supposed to look homemade!

I am proud to say I'm a self-taught vegan baker and my treats will always look homemade. My style is rustic and it has been ever since I started baking cookies as an enthusiastic eleven-year-old. I have been baking cookies for many years now, thousands of cookies, but it wasn't until I started baking vegan cookies seven years ago that I really began to love cookie baking again. I felt the same enthusiasm and joy I experienced when I was younger, when everything was new.

It is with this enthusiasm that I created the most mouthwatering vegan cookies for you. I hope you will enjoy them as much as I do and I hope you will want to bake them again and again to keep your cookie monster happy.

# My All-Time Favorite Cookies

This selection of my absolute favorite cookie recipes is carefully crafted for you. It is a combination of our family-favorite cookies, classic treats from the Nordics with a twist and whimsical and delicious flavor combinations. Berries, chocolates and my favorite spices, cardamom and cinnamon, are all featured in this first chapter.

To begin the chapter I present to you my favorite flavors of all time: blueberries and cardamom. These flavors are united in a cookie that looks like a cute little blueberry pie (page 11).

You will also get a taste of my Crispy Chocolate Chip Cookies (page 12), which are a classic in my house with a clever cashew cream and coconut oil mixture that creates the unique texture and flavor of the cookie.

And who would ever guess the creative ingredients in an indulgent White Chocolate Chip Square Cookie (page 15)? I snuck in some white beans and cashew butter for a yummy fudgy texture.

We also eat rainbows! A colorful batch of Rainbow Shortbread Cookies (page 20) will surely make anyone happy.

The last recipes in this chapter take you on a little journey to my childhood. I am honored to share with you some Nordic classics: my Grandma Martha's Lace Cookies (page 23) and my mother's traditional cinnamon cookies veganized (Donut Cookies, page 27). Also featured in this chapter are the traditional lush Nordic semla bun treats in cookie form (Semla Bun Sandwich Cookies, page 24) and last but not least a festive holiday Gingerbread Sugar Cookie with an irresistible sugar coating (page 29).

# Blueberry Pie Cookies

The recipe for these Blueberry Pie Cookies is inspired by my berry forest—our nearby forest is filled with wild blueberries in the summer. These cookies taste like the traditional blueberry pie my mom bakes: a buttery crust with a hint of cardamom. Ground green cardamom together with blueberries is a magical combination, and these cookies are solid proof of it. With this cookie recipe I welcome you to my berry forest, a cozy and beautiful place where you can take a moment to relax: Take a deep breath and then take a big bite of these mini pie cookies.

## Yield: 14 cookies

1 cup (125 g) all-purpose flour

⅓ cup (30 g) rolled oats

¼ cup (50 g) light brown sugar

½ tsp ground cardamom

½ tsp baking powder

¼ tsp baking soda

¼ tsp salt

3 tbsp (45 ml) maple syrup

⅓ cup (70 g) coconut oil, room temperature and scoopable

¼ cup + 1 tbsp (75 g) almond butter

½ cup (70 g) wild blueberries or blueberries (fresh or frozen)

*Tip*: I recommend using wild blueberries, which are also called bilberries, in these cookies, but blueberries work well too, although they have a less intense blueberry flavor.

Preheat the oven to 375°F (190°C). Line a baking sheet with parchment paper.

In a bowl, whisk together the flour, rolled oats, light brown sugar, cardamom, baking powder, baking soda and salt. Add the maple syrup, coconut oil and almond butter, and knead everything into a cookie dough with your hands. The cookie dough should be solid, but it can feel a bit crumbly at this point.

Scoop about 1½ tablespoons (22 g) of the cookie dough and flatten the cookies on the parchment paper so that they are 2½ inches (6 cm) in diameter. If the cookie dough feels too dry and crumbly, use wet or oiled hands to flatten the cookies.

Roughly divide the blueberries for each cookie and press them gently into the middle of each cookie. If you are using large blueberries instead of smaller wild blueberries, you can cut them in half before placing them on the cookie.

Bake the cookies for 8 to 10 minutes, or until the cookies turn golden brown.

Let the cookies cool for 15 minutes on the baking sheet before moving them onto a cooling rack. Enjoy the cookies either slightly warm when they are still soft or the next day when they are crunchier.

Store the cookies in an airtight container at room temperature for up to 3 days or in the refrigerator for up to 6 days. The cookies will harden in the refrigerator due to the coconut oil, so let the cookies sit at room temperature for 15 to 30 minutes before eating to allow the flavors to settle.

# Crispy Chocolate Chip Cookies

Baking is science. Getting the right combination of ingredients together for an unforgettable cookie experience is what prompted me to make this recipe. I discovered that using soaked and blended cashews and coconut oil as the "butter" of the cookie gives an incredibly delicious texture to the cookie. These cookies are crispy and crunchy and beautifully caramel-flavored thanks to the coconut sugar.

## Yield: 12-15 cookies

⅔ cup (100 g) cashews, unsalted and not roasted

1 cup (125 g) all-purpose flour

¾ cup (135 g) coconut sugar

½ tsp baking soda

¼ tsp salt

¼ cup (70 g) coconut oil, room temperature and scoopable

¾ cup (130 g) vegan chocolate chips

1-2 tbsp (15-30 ml) plant-based milk such as oat milk, optional

Tips: Try this cookie with ¾ cup (130 g) of vegan milk chocolate or vegan white chocolate chunks for an even sweeter treat!

You can also use ⅔ cup (145 g) of light brown sugar instead of ¾ cup (135 g) of coconut sugar to make the cookies.

Soak the cashews for 15 minutes in a bowl filled with hot, just-boiled water so that all the cashews are under water.

Preheat the oven to 375°F (190°C). Line two baking sheets with parchment paper.

In a bowl, mix together the flour, coconut sugar, baking soda and salt.

Rinse and drain the soaked cashews well and blend them together with the coconut oil. You might have to scrape the cashews and coconut oil from the edges of the blender a few times when blending.

Keep blending for 2 to 4 minutes, or until you have a smooth, buttery mixture. It's okay to have some tiny bits and pieces of cashews in the mixture.

Combine the "butter" mixture with the dry ingredients and mix with a spoon until everything is combined.

Add the chocolate chips and knead the dough with your hands until the cookie dough is solid. If the cookie dough is too crumbly at this point, add plant-based milk ½ tablespoon (7 ml) at a time until the cookie dough sticks together.

Scoop about 2 tablespoons (30 g) of the cookie dough and flatten each into a round cookie with a diameter of about 2½ inches (6 cm).

Bake in the oven for 8 to 10 minutes, or until the cookies are golden brown and crispy on the edges. Let the cookies cool on the baking sheet for at least 15 minutes before moving them onto a cooling rack.

Store the cookies in an airtight container at room temperature for up to 5 days or in the refrigerator for up to 8 days. The cookies will harden in the refrigerator due to the coconut oil.

# White Chocolate Chip Square Cookies

Have you ever tried beans in baked cookies? If you haven't tried this yet, I'm encouraging you to give it a go with a family-favorite recipe. White beans work like magic in vegan cookies, making them chewy and soft together with smooth cashew butter— and they're impossible to taste! These delicious squares contain only a small amount of flour to ensure maximum fudginess. I like to use gluten-free oat flour to make these cookies gluten-free, but you can use ⅓ cup (40 g) of all-purpose flour as well.

## Yield: 16 square cookies

⅓ cup (65 g) cooked white beans (Cannellini, Great Northern or Navy beans)

⅓ cup (85 g) smooth cashew butter (see Tip)

3 tbsp (40 g) coconut oil, room temperature and scoopable

⅓ cup (60 g) coconut sugar or light brown sugar

¼ cup (25 g) gluten-free oat flour

¼ tsp salt

⅓ cup (60 g) chopped vegan white chocolate or vegan white chocolate chips

Preheat the oven to 350°F (180°C). Line an 8 x 8-inch (20 x 20-cm) baking pan with parchment paper.

In a food processor, blend the white beans, cashew butter, coconut oil and coconut sugar into a smooth mixture. In a separate bowl, mix together the oat flour and salt.

Combine the dry ingredients with the wet ingredients and fold in the chopped white chocolate pieces or chips. The cookie dough is supposed to be sticky.

Flatten the cookie dough into the baking pan. If the dough is too sticky, use wet fingertips to press the dough.

Bake for 15 to 20 minutes, or until golden brown. Remove the cookies from the oven and let them cool in the pan for 15 minutes before moving to a cooling rack. The cookies are very soft straight from the oven but firm up on the cooling rack. Cut the cookies into squares when they are cooled.

Store the cookies at room temperature in an airtight container for up to 4 days or in the refrigerator for up to a week.

Tip: Cashew butter is easy to make at home! Toast 2 to 4 cups (340 to 680 g) of cashews on a baking sheet lined with parchment paper at 375°F (190°C) for about 5 to 8 minutes, or until they start browning a bit. Just make sure not to burn them. Blend all the toasted cashews in a high-speed blender or food processor until you have a smooth nut butter. This takes about 5 to 10 minutes depending on the blender. You might need to scrape the ground nuts from the edges of the blender several times during the blending process. Sometimes you need to let the blender rest in between blending for a good 15 minutes so as not to overheat the machine.

# Crunchy Peanut Butter Cookies

With a fun crunch from corn flakes and a lovely chewy texture from peanut butter, these Crunchy Peanut Butter Cookies are the perfect sweet treat for all peanut butter lovers. The cookie dough itself is so tasty, I sometimes save a few cookie dough balls to enjoy as a raw treat while waiting for the rest of the cookies to bake. Try this cookie with cashew butter if you are not a peanut butter fan.

## Yield: 16 cookies

1 tbsp (8 g) ground flax seeds

2½ tbsp (37.5 ml) water

1 cup (40 g) corn flakes

½ cup (100 g) granulated sugar

⅓ cup (40 g) all-purpose flour

¼ tsp baking soda

¼ tsp salt

¾ cup (190 g) smooth peanut butter

2 tbsp (30 ml) plant-based milk such as oat milk

Preheat the oven to 350°F (180°C). Line two baking sheets with parchment paper.

Make a vegan "egg" in a small bowl by mixing together the ground flax seeds and water until the mixture thickens. Set it aside.

In a bowl, whisk together the corn flakes, granulated sugar, flour, baking soda and salt.

With your hands, combine the peanut butter, flax "egg" and dry ingredient mixture until you have a solid dough. Add the plant-based milk and roll the dough into 16 balls.

Flatten each ball on the parchment paper into a thin cookie with a diameter of about 2½ inches (6 cm).

Bake the cookies for 10 minutes and let them cool for 10 minutes on the baking sheet before moving them onto a cooling rack.

Store the cookies in an airtight container at room temperature for up to 3 days and in the refrigerator for up to a week.

# Cinnamon Roll Sugar Cookies

A classic sugar cookie turns into an irresistible cinnamon roll-flavored treat with just a few easy steps! Make the dough as you would in baking a classic sugar cookie. You don't need to chill the dough; just flatten two layers of sugar cookie dough into a baking pan. And don't forget the key ingredient: a crunchy cinnamon and brown sugar mixture combined with a little bit of cookie dough between the two layers. This is the secret to making these cute melt-in-your-mouth sugar cookie squares taste like sweet cinnamon rolls!

### Yield: 24 square cookies

1¼ cups (160 g) all-purpose flour

½ tsp baking powder

¼ tsp salt

½ cup (115 g) vegan butter, room temperature

½ cup (100 g) granulated sugar

¼ cup (50 g) light brown sugar

1 tbsp (8 g) cinnamon

Tip: If you are using a different-sized baking pan, please adjust the baking time. With a bigger pan, the cookie is thinner and bakes faster.

Preheat the oven to 350°F (180°C). Line a 5½ x 7½-inch (14 x 19-cm) baking pan with parchment paper.

In a bowl, whisk together the flour, baking powder and salt. In another bowl with a handheld mixer or with a stand mixer, beat the vegan butter and granulated sugar together until creamy.

Combine the dry ingredients with the creamed butter and sugar mixture. Mix them together with a wooden spoon or a baking spatula until the dough is firm. You can also mix the dough by hand to make it smooth.

Divide the cookie dough into three parts: two 5-ounce (140-g) parts and one smaller 2-ounce (60-g) part. You can also just eyeball the three parts. Press one 5-ounce (140-g) piece of dough into the baking pan.

Mix the small 2-ounce (60-g) piece of dough with the light brown sugar and cinnamon until you have a coarse crumble. Sprinkle it evenly on top of the first layer.

With a rolling pin, roll the second large cookie dough part on a piece of parchment paper or a similar nonstick surface until it's the same size as the first layer. Place the second layer on top of the sugar and cinnamon layer and press the layers gently together.

Bake for 22 to 25 minutes, or until golden and lightly browned. Gently cut into squares after baking while they're still soft and let them cool in the pan for 15 minutes. These cookies are very soft right after baking but will firm up when cooled. Store the cookies in an airtight container at room temperature for up to 5 days or in the refrigerator for up to 10 days.

# Rainbow Shortbread Cookies

A buttery shortbread cookie covered in a beautiful sugary rainbow—this is a cookie to bring joy and happiness to your day. The shortbread cookie is easy to make, but the rainbow sugar frosting needs a little bit of patience. The icing is made by whipping confectioners' sugar and aquafaba—the liquid from a can of either chickpeas or white beans—into a fluffy and thick mixture. This mixture is so thick you can pipe it into any shape, such as pretty, happy rainbow stripes. You can save this cookie recipe for a fun occasion or simply to make yourself smile. We all need some sugar and rainbows!

## Yield: 12-15 cookies

⅔ cup (150 g) vegan butter, softened

¼ cup (50 g) light brown sugar

¼ cup (50 g) granulated sugar

1 tsp vanilla extract

1½ cups (190 g) all-purpose flour

¼ tsp salt

### Royal Icing
¼ cup (60 ml) aquafaba (see Tip)

1 tsp lemon juice, or more if needed

3 cups (360 g) confectioners' sugar

Vegan food coloring of your choice

**Tip:** Aquafaba is the liquid from a can of chickpeas or white beans. It can be used as a vegan "egg" in baking, and it is also whippable.

Preheat the oven to 350°F (180°C). Line an 8 x 8-inch (20 x 20-cm) pan with parchment paper so that it is easy to lift the cookie when it is baked.

In a bowl using a handheld mixer or with a stand mixer, cream together the vegan butter, sugars and vanilla extract for 1 to 2 minutes, or until you have a fluffy and creamy mixture.

Add the flour and salt to the creamed butter mixture, and fold everything gently together with a spatula. Knead the dough with your hands until it is solid and firm.

Press the cookie dough into the bottom of the baking pan. Bake it in the oven for 20 minutes, or until the cookie is slightly golden brown. Let the cookie cool in the baking pan for at least 15 minutes.

In a ceramic or glass bowl with a handheld mixer or with a stand mixer, mix the aquafaba and lemon juice until you have a fluffy consistency. This will take about 3 to 5 minutes.

Sift the confectioners' sugar over the aquafaba cream little by little while beating the mixture. Mix it until you have a thick cream that stays in the bowl when you turn it upside down. Add more sugar if needed for the desired consistency. Or add more lemon juice if you need to thin it out.

Divide the icing into various bowls and add the vegan food coloring to each bowl. Mix it with a spoon and pipe each color as a stripe on top of the shortbread cookie. With a sharp knife, cut the cookie into desired pieces and let them dry.

Store the cookies at room temperature in an airtight container for up to 5 days or in the refrigerator for up to 8 days.

# Grandma Martha's Lace Cookies

There is one special cookie that takes me back to my Grandma Martha's kitchen: lace cookies. As a little girl I used to watch her transform basic pantry ingredients into these beautiful thin oat cookies, which were so sweet they satisfied my sweet tooth for a long time—especially when I ate three cookies in a row! Martha's original recipe calls for one egg, but I left it out, and although the texture differs from the original, these vegan lace cookies are just as delicious as my Grandma's. There is one secret ingredient, which I love and which my grandma loved too: ground cardamom. Just half a teaspoon of this flavorful spice brings these basic pantry ingredient cookies to the next level.

## Yield: 14 cookies

⅓ cup (80 g) vegan butter
1 cup (90 g) rolled oats
¼ cup (50 g) light brown sugar
¼ cup (50 g) granulated sugar
2 tbsp (15 g) all-purpose flour
1 tsp baking powder
½ tsp ground cardamom
¼ tsp salt

Preheat the oven to 390°F (200°C). Line two baking sheets with parchment paper.

Warm the butter in a microwave or on the stovetop over low-medium heat until it is very soft, nearly liquid, and let it cool for 5 minutes.

In a large bowl, whisk together the rolled oats, sugars, flour, baking powder, cardamom and salt. Add the butter and mix everything together until you have a solid cookie dough. Let the dough rest for 10 minutes.

Scoop 1½ tablespoons (22 g) of the dough and flatten it into a ⅕-inch (5-mm)-thin cookie about 2½ inches (6 cm) in diameter. Leave space about 2 inches (5 cm) per side for the cookie to spread. Use wet hands to shape the cookie if it is too sticky and crumbly.

Bake the cookies for 5 to 8 minutes, or until they are golden brown.

Let the lace cookies cool on the baking sheet for 15 minutes, or until they are solid enough to move to a cooling rack.

Store the cookies in an airtight container for up to 3 days or in the refrigerator for up to 6 days.

Tip: You can also freeze baked lace cookies. They keep their flavor in the freezer for up to a month, and they also taste delicious straight from the freezer, cold and crispy.

# Semla Bun Sandwich Cookies

A semla bun is a classic Nordic cardamom bun usually eaten in January and February and especially on Shrove Tuesday. This fluffy semla bun is filled with jam and almond paste or a generous dollop of whipped cream. I created this traditional Nordic treat in a quick-to-make cookie form! Instead of a yeast bun dough, which requires time to rise, this cookie dough comes together in mere minutes and can be baked straight away. What makes these cookies special is the ground cardamom, a traditional spice in Nordic buns, and the almond paste sandwiched between two cookies.

## Yield: 9 sandwich cookies

½ cup (115 g) vegan butter, softened

½ cup (100 g) granulated sugar

2 cups (250 g) all-purpose flour

2 tsp (4 g) ground cardamom

½ tsp baking powder

¼ tsp salt

1 tbsp (15 ml) plant-based milk such as oat milk, optional

### Almond Paste
⅓ cup (30 g) almond meal

⅔ cup (80 g) confectioners' sugar

1 tbsp (15 ml) water

½ tsp vanilla extract

### Filling
⅓ cup (80 g) raspberry jam or marmalade

Preheat the oven to 350°F (180°C). Line a baking sheet with parchment paper.

In a bowl with a handheld mixer or with a stand mixer, cream together the vegan butter and granulated sugar for 2 minutes, or until creamy.

In another bowl, combine the flour, cardamom, baking powder and salt. Add the dry ingredients to the wet ingredients little by little, folding the dough gently with a wooden spoon or spatula. Knead with your hands to combine the dough. If the dough feels dry, add the plant-based milk ½ tablespoon (7.5 ml) at a time until you have a solid dough that can easily be formed into balls.

Scoop about 1½ tablespoons (22 g) of the cookie dough and flatten each one on the parchment paper until the cookie is about ½ inch (1 cm) thick and 1½ inches (4 cm) in diameter. Leave about 1 inch (2.5 cm) of space between each cookie.

Bake the cookies for 8 to 10 minutes. The cookies are soft straight from the oven, but they will firm up when you let them cool on the baking sheet for about 15 minutes.

In a bowl, mix together the almond meal, confectioners' sugar, water and vanilla extract. Spread the almond paste mixture and the jam on one cookie and press another cookie gently on top.

These cookies are best when eaten on the same day of baking, but you can also store them in the refrigerator as a sandwich cookie for up to 3 days.

# Donut Cookies

This Donut Cookie recipe is based on a traditional Finnish recipe: the Cinnamon S Cookie. My mother baked these cookies for Christmas every year when I was a little girl. I remember the sweet cinnamon scent lingering in the kitchen. The process of making these cookies is therapeutic: rolling each cookie in a sweet cinnamon-sugar coating before carefully forming the S shape. This time I made a donut version of the classic shape because donuts are more fun and you can go wild with sprinkles or any other festive coating you wish.

## Yield: 20 donut cookies

½ cup (115 g) vegan butter, softened

½ cup (100 g) + 2 tbsp (30 g) granulated sugar, divided

3 tbsp (45 ml) aquafaba (see Tips)

1 tsp vanilla extract

1½ cups (190 g) all-purpose flour

1 tbsp (8 g) cornstarch

½ tsp baking powder

Pinch or about ⅛ tsp salt (not needed if the aquafaba is salted)

Preheat the oven to 390°F (200°C). Line two baking sheets with parchment paper.

In a bowl with a handheld mixer or with a stand mixer, cream together the soft butter and ½ cup (100 g) granulated sugar for about 2 minutes, or until the mixture is fluffy. Add the aquafaba and vanilla and keep on beating until everything is combined for about 30 seconds.

In another bowl, mix together the flour, cornstarch, baking powder and salt. Combine the dry ingredients with the wet ingredients, gently folding the dough together with a spoon or spatula.

Knead the dough with your hands until it is easy to handle and doesn't stick to your hands.

Divide the dough into four parts, about 3.5 ounces (100 g) per part.

(continued)

# Donut Cookies (Continued)

½ tbsp (4 g) ground cinnamon

2 tbsp (20 g) vegan sprinkles

On a big plate, mix and spread the cinnamon and 2 tablespoons (30 g) of sugar. Spread the vegan sprinkles on another big plate.

Roll each part of the dough until it is 21 inches (55 cm). Cut the roll into 5 pieces.

Roll each piece in just the cinnamon and sugar or both cinnamon and sugar and vegan sprinkles.

Shape each roll into a donut shape by joining and pressing the ends together on the baking sheet. The hole in the middle should be about 1 inch (2.5 cm) in diameter. Leave about 1½ inches (4 cm) of room for each cookie on each side to spread. Sprinkle more cinnamon and sugar on top of each cookie.

Bake the baking sheets one at a time for 8 minutes. Let the cookies cool on the baking sheet for 15 minutes before moving them onto a cooling rack.

Store the cookies in an airtight container for up to 5 days.

*Tips:* Aquafaba is the liquid from a can of chickpeas or white beans. It can be used as a vegan "egg." Three tablespoons (45 ml) of aquafaba can be used in place of one egg.

You can also make small donut cookies by rolling the dough even thinner and cutting a shorter piece of the dough. The baking time might be a little less for small donut cookies, so check the cookies after 5 minutes of baking.

# Gingerbread Sugar Cookies

Gingerbread Sugar Cookies are a happy and delicious mixture of a traditional Finnish gingerbread recipe and all the gingerbread cookie experiments I have made during several years as a vegan baker. The first gingerbread cookie I created was a raw gingerbread cookie with almond butter. I love the nutty flavor almond butter gives to cookies, and it was a given to include almond butter in this recipe too. When it comes to spices, I wanted to follow a more Finnish gingerbread spice profile, which means ground cardamom is a must! The method of making these cookies is similar to the Finnish tradition: first simmering syrup and butter with the aromatic spices and then mixing this with the dry ingredients. What makes these cookies special—and not very traditional—is the generous coating of sugar.

## Yield: about 75 cookies

⅓ cup (75 g) vegan butter

¾ cup (165 g) light brown sugar

⅓ cup (80 ml) maple syrup

1 tbsp (15 ml) molasses

4 tsp (10 g) ground cinnamon

3 tsp (6 g) ground cardamom

1 tsp ground ginger

¼ tsp cloves

⅓ cup (80 g) almond butter

3 cups (375 g) all-purpose flour

1 tsp baking powder

½ tsp baking soda

½ tsp salt

½ cup (120 ml) vegan cream such as oat or soy-based cooking cream or creamy coconut milk

⅓ cup (70 g) granulated sugar

Preheat the oven to 375°F (190°C). Line a baking sheet with parchment paper.

Warm the vegan butter, light brown sugar, maple syrup, molasses, cinnamon, cardamom, ginger and cloves in a saucepan, constantly stirring for a minute or two. Bring the mixture to a boil, stirring so that it won't burn. Take it off of the heat. Combine the warm sugary mixture with the almond butter and stir well. Let the mixture cool for at least 10 minutes.

In another bowl, mix together the all-purpose flour, baking powder, baking soda and salt.

When the sugary mixture has cooled down, mix it with the dry ingredients. Knead with your hands to get a solid dough. Add the vegan cream little by little to get a solid and firm dough. The dough should be easy to shape and roll.

You can wrap the dough in plastic wrap and store it in the refrigerator until the next day, or you can bake the cookies right away.

Spread the granulated sugar evenly on a large plate.

(continued)

# Gingerbread Sugar Cookies (Continued)

Divide the dough into four parts and roll each part into a ⅕-inch (5-mm)-thick dough. Cut out the cookies using a cookie cutter that is about 1½ inches (4 cm) in diameter and coat both sides of the cookie in sugar.

Bake the cookies in the oven for 7 to 10 minutes. The longer you bake these cookies, the crispier they become. We prefer softer gingerbread cookies, so the baking time is usually 7 minutes. Move them from the baking sheet to a cooling rack immediately or after a few minutes of cooling.

Repeat the process until you have baked all the cookies. You can also save some dough to bake later. Store the cookie dough in the refrigerator for up to 4 days.

Store the cookies in an airtight container at room temperature for up to a week.

*Tips:* Instead of coating each cookie with sugar before baking, you can also decorate the cookies with royal icing. See the recipe for Royal Icing on page 20.

If you use larger cookie cutters the yield might be only about 50 cookies, depending on the size of the cookie cutter.

# Chocolate Lover's Cookies

This chapter is dedicated to all chocolate lovers. Whether you enjoy a classic chocolate chip cookie (Milk Chocolate Chip Cookies, page 35), a mint-flavored chocolate cookie (Mint Chocolate Sandwich Cookies, page 43) or a melt-in-your-mouth double chocolate cookie (Fudgy Double Chocolate Cookies, page 50), I have your sweetest chocolate cravings covered!

Chocolate is my favorite cookie ingredient, and it is the one ingredient that made me fall in love with baking at a young age. I was eleven when I learned to bake a classic chocolate chip cookie, and I have baked thousands of similar cookies since.

Baking vegan chocolate cookies inspires me to be creative with my cookie ingredients. I can slather a gigantic cookie with a gooey peanut butter sauce to make the perfect Chocolate Chip Peanut Butter Cookie Pizza (page 45). I can go wild and use pumpkin purée or sweet potato purée in my chocolate cookie dough, because why not, if it tastes amazing and gives a luscious soft texture?

Then again, I can also make classic chocolate chip cookies almost the same way I baked them in my childhood by just replacing nonvegan ingredients with vegan butter and flax "eggs." Baking vegan chocolate cookies can be easy!

In this chapter, I will take you on a delicious journey exploring vegan chocolate cookies. I hope you will enjoy all the different textures from crunchy to fudgy, crispy to gooey and the various chocolate flavors of these ten decadent and irresistible chocolate cookies.

Enjoy and take a bite, or perhaps dunk your chocolate chip cookie in cold plant-based milk before you do!

# Milk Chocolate Chip Cookies

If you are looking for a traditional chocolate chip cookie recipe, you don't need to look further. These scrumptious cookies are loved by everyone, and no one can ever believe they're vegan. What makes these cookies so special but still traditional? A mixture of ground flax seeds and applesauce becomes the vegan "egg" holding the ingredients together. A high-quality vegan butter is a must for these cookies. I recommend the "butteriest" dairy-free butter you can find because the buttery flavor is an important part of the cookie, as is the vegan milk chocolate. Choose a vegan milk chocolate bar you really love and cut it into chunks.

### Yield: 20 cookies

1 tbsp (10 g) ground flax seeds

3 tbsp (45 g) applesauce

1½ cup (190 g) all-purpose flour

1 tsp baking powder

½ tsp baking soda

½ tsp salt

½ cup (115 g) vegan butter, softened

½ cup (100 g) light brown sugar

½ cup (100 g) granulated sugar

1 cup (140 g) vegan milk chocolate chunks

Tip: If you want, you can chill the dough for 30 minutes in the refrigerator before baking. Chilling the dough makes the butter colder so the cookies do not spread so much. My family and I love these cookies flatter, chewy on the inside and crispy on the edges, so we usually do not chill the cookie dough.

Preheat the oven to 350°F (180°C). Line two baking sheets with parchment paper.

Make the vegan "egg" by mixing the ground flax seeds and applesauce together until fully combined.

In a bowl, whisk together the flour, baking powder, baking soda and salt.

In another bowl with a handheld mixer or with a stand mixer, cream together the vegan butter and the sugars for about 2 minutes. Add the flax "egg" and continue beating the mixture for about 30 seconds.

Sift the dry ingredients over the wet ingredients and gently fold the mixture together with a spatula. Do not overmix the dough. Fold in the vegan milk chocolate chunks.

Scoop about 2 tablespoons (30 g) of cookie dough per cookie and flatten it into a cookie shape. Usually about 10 cookies fit on the baking sheet perfectly. I recommend baking one sheet at a time for the best results.

Bake the cookies for 10 to 12 minutes, or until the cookies are golden brown on the edges. Let the cookies cool completely, for about 15 to 20 minutes, before moving them onto a cooling rack.

Store the cookies in an airtight container either at room temperature for up to 3 days or in the refrigerator for up to 5 days. The cookies will become firmer in the refrigerator, so you can take them out about 20 minutes before serving them if you want them softer.

# Oatmeal Chocolate Chip Cookies

Oatmeal Chocolate Chip Cookies are cozy. They are a cup of hot chocolate enjoyed on a cold day by the fireplace. They are fluffy soft socks and flannel pajamas. They are the sweetest hugs and cuddles. These cookies are soft and more wholesome than regular chocolate chip cookies, with rolled oats and good quality dark chocolate. Enjoy them warm with a glass of cold oat milk or enjoy them cold with a glass of hot chocolate.

## Yield: 34 cookies

1 tbsp (10 g) chia seeds

3 tbsp (45 ml) water

1½ cups (190 g) all-purpose flour

1 tsp baking powder

½ tsp baking soda

½ tsp salt

¾ cup (170 g) vegan butter, softened

¾ cup (170 g) light brown sugar

1 tsp vanilla extract

1½ cups (130 g) rolled oats

1 cup (140 g) vegan dark chocolate chunks (70-80% dark chocolate)

Preheat the oven to 350°F (180°C). Line two baking sheets with parchment paper.

In a small bowl, whisk together the chia seeds and water and set the mixture aside.

In a large bowl, whisk together the flour, baking powder, baking soda and salt.

In a bowl with a handheld mixer or with a stand mixer, cream together the vegan butter, light brown sugar and vanilla extract for about 2 minutes, or until you have a creamy and fluffy consistency. Add the chia "egg" and continue beating the mixture for about 30 seconds.

Sift the dry ingredients over the wet ingredients and gently fold them together with a spatula. Do not overmix the dough. Fold in the rolled oats and vegan dark chocolate chunks.

With a cookie scoop or tablespoon, scoop about 1 tablespoon (20 g) per cookie and flatten it just a little. Place the cookies about 1½ inches (4 cm) apart from each other on the baking sheet.

Bake the sheets one at a time for 10 to 12 minutes and let the cookies cool for 10 minutes on the baking sheet before moving them onto a cooling rack.

Store the cookies in an airtight container at room temperature for up to 4 days, or in the refrigerator for up to a week. If you store them in the refrigerator, warm the cookies for a minute or two in the oven if you want them to be warm and gooey.

# Mocha Chocolate Chip Cookies

This is a cookie for all the coffee and cookie lovers; the perfect treat for a little afternoon pick-me-up is a Mocha Chocolate Chip Cookie. This sweet cookie is full of rich flavor from both instant coffee and dark chocolate—a friendly pair creating the delicious mocha flavor. The cookies are sweetened with both confectioners' sugar and light brown sugar, giving them a yummy chewy texture. Enjoy this cookie with a cup of coffee to intensify the mocha flavor.

## Yield: 22 cookies

1¼ cups (155 g) all-purpose flour

¾ cup (90 g) confectioners' sugar

¼ cup (25 g) cocoa powder

2 tbsp (8 g) instant coffee

1 tsp baking soda

¼ tsp salt

½ cup (115 g) vegan butter

⅓ cup (70 g) light brown sugar

3 tbsp (45 ml) aquafaba (see Tip)

¾ cup (130 g) vegan dark chocolate chunks

In a bowl, whisk together the flour, confectioners' sugar, cocoa powder, instant coffee, baking soda and salt.

In a bowl with a handheld mixer or with a stand mixer, cream together the vegan butter and the light brown sugar for about 2 minutes until they are creamy and fluffy. Add the aquafaba and keep on beating until everything is combined, about 30 seconds.

Add the dry ingredients to the creamed butter and sugar and fold everything gently together. Don't overmix the dough. Fold in the chocolate chunks and chill the dough for 30 minutes.

Preheat the oven to 350°F (180°C). Line two baking sheets with parchment paper.

Scoop about 1½ tablespoons (25 g) of the cookie dough, roll it into a ball and flatten it a bit on the parchment paper.

Bake about 10 cookies at a time on one baking sheet for 10 minutes.

Let the cookies cool on the baking sheet for 15 minutes before moving them onto a cooling rack.

Store the cookies in an airtight container at room temperature for up to 4 days, or in the refrigerator for up to a week.

Tip: Aquafaba is the liquid from a can of chickpeas or white beans. It can be used as a vegan "egg." Three tablespoons (45 ml) of aquafaba can be used in place of 1 egg.

# Chocolate Chip Pumpkin Cookies

When you're craving dessert, may I suggest these utterly delicious Chocolate Chip Pumpkin Cookies with vegan vanilla ice cream sandwiched in between? What makes these cookies special is the pumpkin purée and cinnamon flavors. These soft cookies are perfect as sandwich cookies, but of course you can eat them without ice cream too. I recommend enjoying all of these cookies on the same day you bake them, when they are at their softest.

## Yield: 12 sandwich cookies

2 cups (260 g) all-purpose flour

½ cup (100 g) light brown sugar

1 tsp cinnamon

½ tsp baking soda

¼ tsp salt

⅓ cup (80 g) pumpkin purée (see Tips)

⅓ cup (80 ml) maple syrup

¼ cup (55 g) coconut oil or vegan butter, softened

¾ cup (120 g) vegan chocolate chunks

1 cup (about 150 g) vegan vanilla ice cream

In a bowl, mix together the flour, light brown sugar, cinnamon, baking soda and salt. Add the pumpkin purée, syrup and coconut oil and fold them gently together. Fold the chocolate chunks into the dough and roll the dough into a big ball. Chill the cookie dough in the refrigerator, covered in plastic wrap, for 30 minutes.

Preheat the oven to 350°F (180°C). Line two baking sheets with parchment paper.

Scoop about 2 tablespoons (30 g) of the cookie dough and press it gently onto the baking sheet.

Bake the cookies for 8 to 10 minutes and let them cool on the baking sheet for 15 minutes before moving them onto a cooling rack.

Once the cookies have cooled, spread the vegan vanilla ice cream between two cookies and enjoy!

Store the cookies (with no ice cream) in an airtight container for 1 to 2 days. If they are stored for longer, the cookies harden and are not convenient as ice cream sandwich cookies.

Tips: To make an even sweeter dessert, swirl homemade caramel sauce into the vanilla ice cream. Just mix ¼ cup (60 g) nut butter, 3 tablespoons (45 ml) maple syrup and a pinch of salt together to make the caramel.

Making homemade pumpkin purée is easy: Steam half of a small pumpkin or one quarter of a large pumpkin at a time, then mash the soft pieces with a fork and store what you don't use in the freezer in ⅓-cup (80-g) portions. This way you have pumpkin purée in the freezer whenever you feel like baking cookies! Take the purée out of the freezer a few hours before baking.

# Mint Chocolate Sandwich Cookies

A classic flavor combination, chocolate and mint make a perfect match in these cute cookies. With their dark chocolate cookies and creamy mint fillings, these cookies remind me of a childhood favorite: mint chocolate Domino. The Domino cookie is like the Oreo cookie, and they are a classic here in Finland.

Making these heart-shaped sandwich cookies requires patience: The cookie dough needs to be softened and flattened with the palms of your hands first to ensure that it does not crumble. If it does, just patch it up and continue. Roll the dough little by little, patiently. The reward will come: cute and sweet heart-shaped mint cookies to melt anyone's heart.

## Yield: 25 sandwich cookies

⅓ cup (55 g) dark chocolate chips

1 cup (125 g) all-purpose flour

½ cup (60 g) confectioners' sugar

¼ cup (25 g) cocoa powder

¼ tsp baking soda

¼ tsp salt

¼ cup (55 g) coconut oil, room temperature and scoopable

3 tbsp (45 ml) plant-based milk such as oat milk

Preheat the oven to 350°F (180°C). Line two baking sheets with parchment paper.

Melt the dark chocolate chips on the stovetop by first filling a saucepan with about 1 inch (2.5 cm) of water. Place the chocolate in a heatproof bowl on top of the saucepan. Make sure the bowl is not touching the water and that no water gets in the chocolate bowl (or else the chocolate will become lumpy). Warm the chocolate over medium heat, stirring for about 2 minutes, or until the chocolate is smooth. Set the melted chocolate aside.

In a bowl, mix together the flour, confectioners' sugar, cocoa powder, baking soda and salt. Add the melted chocolate and coconut oil to the dry ingredients and mix to form a crumbly dough. Add the plant-based milk 1 tablespoon (15 ml) at a time and knead with your hands to make a firm dough.

Flatten one-third of the dough with the palm of your hand and roll it with a rolling pin into a ¼-inch (6-mm) sheet of dough. The dough can feel crumbly, but just press it with your hand gently together if it crumbles.

(continued)

# Mint Chocolate Sandwich Cookies (Continued)

**Cookie Filling**

½ cup (60 g) confectioners' sugar

2 tbsp (30 g) coconut oil, room temperature and scoopable

½ tsp peppermint extract

⅛–¼ tsp spirulina powder

Make the cookies with a small cookie cutter (about 2 x 1½ inches [4.5 x 3.5 cm]) and move them to a baking sheet with a thin spatula. You don't need to leave much room for the cookies; they won't spread a lot. Repeat this process with the rest of the dough.

Bake the cookies for 5 minutes and let them cool on the baking sheet for 15 minutes before moving them onto a cooling rack. Let them cool completely before filling them.

In a bowl, mix together the confectioners' sugar, coconut oil, peppermint extract and spirulina powder with a spoon.

Spread the mint cream carefully on a cookie and press another cookie on top. Repeat the process until you have filled all the cookies. Store the cookies in the refrigerator for about 30 minutes to make the cream filling firm.

Store the cookies in an airtight container in the refrigerator for up to a week.

# Chocolate Chip Peanut Butter Cookie Pizza

Chocolate Chip Peanut Butter Cookie Pizza is like a gooey-in-the-middle, crispy-on-the-edges cookie. This cookie is perhaps the only one that you won't mind sharing with others because it is enormous. The secret to the gooeyness of this cookie pizza is a peanut butter layer slathered between two layers of dough before baking that melts when the cookie is baked. You can enjoy this giant cookie either warm, when it is still soft and gooey, or after a few hours or overnight when it has firmed up and is easy to cut into cookie pizza slices.

## Yield: 1 (10-inch [25-cm]) pizza cookie

1 tbsp (8 g) ground flax seeds

3 tbsp (45 ml) plant-based milk such as oat milk

½ cup (120 g) smooth unsweetened peanut butter

¼ cup (60 ml) maple syrup

¾ tsp salt, divided

½ cup (115 g) vegan butter, softened

½ cup (100 g) light brown sugar

Preheat the oven to 375°F (190°C). Line a large baking sheet (about 16 x 14 inches [40 x 35 cm]) with parchment paper.

In a bowl, mix together the ground flax seeds and plant-based milk to form a flax "egg" and set the mixture aside.

In another bowl, mix together the peanut butter, maple syrup and ¼ teaspoon of salt until you have a smooth peanut butter caramel.

In a bowl with a handheld mixer or with a stand mixer, cream together the softened vegan butter and light brown sugar for at least 2 minutes. Add the flax "egg" and continue beating for a minute.

(continued)

1½ cups (190 g) all-purpose flour

½ tsp baking powder

½ tsp baking soda

1 cup (170 g) vegan chocolate chips

In another bowl, whisk together the flour, baking powder, baking soda and ½ teaspoon of salt.

Combine the dry ingredients with the creamed butter, sugar and flax "egg" mixture. Mix the ingredients together until you have a firm cookie dough batter. Fold in the chocolate chips and knead with your hands to get a firm dough.

Flatten about half of the cookie dough into a round pizza shape that is about 9½ inches (24 cm) in diameter.

Spread the peanut butter caramel evenly on top of the pizza. Add the second cookie dough layer on top of the peanut butter caramel layer. The peanut butter will spread a bit from the edges, but you can fold it in with the cookie dough edges.

Bake the cookie pizza in the oven for 12 to 15 minutes. With 12 minutes of baking time, you will have a soft and gooey cookie pizza. The more you bake the cookie pizza, the less gooey it becomes.

Store the cookie pizza well covered at room temperature for up to 3 days so that it stays soft. If you want it to be firmer and also easier to slice, store it in the refrigerator for up to 6 days.

# Hazelnut Chocolate Cookies

Chopped hazelnuts and chocolate make a delicious vegan "Nutella"-flavored chocolate chip cookie. This Hazelnut Chocolate Cookie recipe is an old one from my friend's mother, who received it from her friend over 30 years ago. This cookie is among the first ones I baked as an enthusiastic eleven-year-old, and I am glad to share the veganized version of this classic recipe with you. This cookie is similar to my Milk Chocolate Chip Cookie (page 35), but it is not as sweet due to the dark chocolate used. The hazelnuts give an exquisite and unique flavor to these thin melt-in-your-mouth cookies.

## Yield: 28 cookies

1 tbsp (8 g) ground flax seeds

2½ tbsp (38 ml) water

1 cup (125 g) all-purpose flour

½ tsp baking soda

½ tsp salt

½ cup (115 g) vegan butter, softened

½ cup (100 g) granulated sugar

¼ cup (50 g) light brown sugar

¾ cup (120 g) vegan chocolate chunks

½ cup (60 g) chopped hazelnuts

**Tip:** If you prefer your cookies thicker, try chilling the cookie dough for 30 minutes. The cookies will spread less, and the result will be a thicker and chunkier cookie.

Preheat the oven to 350°F (180°C). Line two baking sheets with parchment paper.

In a bowl, mix together the ground flax seeds and water to make a vegan "egg." Set the mixture aside.

In another bowl, whisk together the flour, baking soda and salt.

In a bowl with a handheld mixer or with a stand mixer, cream together the vegan butter and sugars for about 2 minutes, or until they are creamy and fluffy. Add the flax "egg" and continue beating the mixture for about 30 seconds.

Sift the dry ingredients onto the creamed butter and sugar and fold everything gently together. Don't overmix the dough. Fold in the chocolate chunks and the chopped hazelnuts.

Scoop about 1 tablespoon (15 g) of the cookie dough and flatten it on the parchment paper into a cookie shape. If you want to make the cookies even in size and shape, take a 2-inch (5-cm) in diameter round cookie cutter, press each flattened cookie through the cutter and use the leftover edges to form the next cookie.

Bake 14 cookies at a time on one baking sheet for 10 to 12 minutes, or until the edges start to brown.

Let the cookies cool on the baking sheet for 15 minutes before moving them onto a cooling rack.

Store the cookies in an airtight container at room temperature for up to 3 days, or in the refrigerator for up to a week.

# Fudgy Double Chocolate Cookies

These Fudgy Double Chocolate Cookies melt in your mouth and are very sweet thanks to two sweeteners in the cookie dough—sugar and maple syrup—and the extra dusting of confectioners' sugar. This cookie is similar to a crinkle cookie, but what makes it special is the two chocolates it contains: vegan dark chocolate and vegan milk chocolate. The texture of the cookie is quite soft and fudgy, and the flavor is rich and chocolatey, just like a double chocolate cookie should be.

## Yield: 24 cookies

⅓ cup (55 g) dark chocolate chips

¼ cup + 2 tbsp (80 g) coconut oil, room temperature and scoopable

¼ cup (60 g) almond butter

⅓ cup (70 g) granulated sugar

¼ cup (60 ml) maple syrup

1 cup (125 g) all-purpose flour

¼ cup (25 g) cocoa powder

½ tsp baking powder

¼ tsp baking soda

¼ tsp salt

½–2 tbsp (7.5-30 ml) plant-based milk such as oat milk

½ cup (85 g) vegan milk chocolate chunks

1-2 tbsp (8-16 g) confectioners' sugar

Preheat the oven to 350°F (180°C). Line two baking sheets with parchment paper.

Melt the dark chocolate chips on the stovetop by first filling a saucepan with about 1 inch (2.5 cm) of water. Place the chocolate in a heatproof bowl on top of the saucepan. Make sure the bowl is not touching the water and that no water gets in the chocolate bowl (or else the chocolate will become lumpy). Warm the chocolate over medium heat, stirring for about 2 minutes, or until the chocolate is smooth. Set the melted chocolate aside.

Add the coconut oil, almond butter, granulated sugar and maple syrup to the melted chocolate and mix everything together.

In another bowl, whisk together the flour, cocoa powder, baking powder, baking soda and salt. Combine the wet ingredients with the dry ingredients and knead them into a dough. Add the plant-based milk ½ tablespoon (about 10 ml) at a time until the dough is easy to handle. Fold in the vegan milk chocolate chunks.

Scoop about 1½ to 2 tablespoons (15 to 22 g) of the cookie dough and roll it into a ball. Flatten it slightly on the parchment paper.

Bake 12 cookies at a time on one baking sheet for 10 minutes. Let the cookies cool on the baking sheet for 15 minutes before moving them onto a cooling rack. With a fine sifter, dust the cookies with the confectioners' sugar.

Store the cookies in an airtight container at room temperature for up to 5 days.

# Double Chocolate Skillet Cookie

Vegan baking is more than just vegan butter, sugar and flour combined into a dough. Vegan baking means experimenting with fun—even surprising—simple ingredients to achieve something special. This is the case with the Double Chocolate Skillet Cookie, a pie-like cookie, baked in a skillet and containing sweet potato purée! To make a gooey caramel, just stir sweet potato purée with sugar and butter in a warm skillet and then combine this warm mixture with the dry ingredients. Add chocolate chunks and bake it in the oven.

## Yield: 1 skillet cookie

1 cup (220 g) light brown sugar

½ cup (135 g) sweet potato purée

½ cup (120 g) cashew butter

1 tsp vanilla extract

2 cups (250 g) all-purpose flour

¼ cup (25 g) cocoa powder

1 tsp baking powder

½ tsp baking soda

½ tsp salt

¼ cup (60 ml) plant-based milk such as oat milk

½ cup (85 g) vegan white chocolate chunks

½ cup (85 g) vegan dark chocolate chopped into tiny pieces

2 cups (300 g) vegan vanilla ice cream or 1 cup (250 ml) vegan whipped cream

Preheat the oven to 350°F (180°C).

On the stovetop in an 8½-inch (22-cm) greased cast iron skillet over low-medium heat, warm the sugar, sweet potato purée, cashew butter and vanilla extract, constantly stirring for about 2 minutes, or until you have a gooey caramel mixture. Set it aside to cool down for 5 minutes.

In a bowl, whisk together the flour, cocoa powder, baking powder, baking soda and salt.

Combine the caramel mixture and the plant-based milk with the dry ingredients and fold them together with a wooden spoon or spatula. Fold in the vegan chocolate pieces.

You can bake the cookie in the same skillet you used to warm the caramel mixture. Grease the skillet with a little oil or vegan butter. Press the cookie dough onto the bottom of the skillet and bake it on the middle rack of the oven for 20 to 25 minutes. Check the cookie with a toothpick from the center after 20 minutes. If a lot of raw cookie dough sticks to the toothpick, bake it for another 5 minutes. The cookie is supposed to be a bit gooey when you take it out of the oven, but not too raw.

Let the cookie cool in the skillet for about 15 minutes. Enjoy the skillet cookie with vegan ice cream or vegan whipped cream.

To store the cookie, cut it into pieces with a wooden spatula and store it in an airtight container at room temperature for up to 4 days, or in the refrigerator for up to a week.

# Chocolate Chip Shortbread

A classic buttery shortbread cookie is taken to the next level in the simplest way: by adding chocolate chips! This shortbread recipe is easy: Cream butter and sugar and add flour and salt. Add the flour to make a buttery dough and fold in the chocolate chips last. Then press the dough into a baking tin and bake it. Once this treat is out of the oven, poke holes in it with a fork to make the classic shortbread cookie look. Then you can cut the cookie into cute rectangular shortbreads.

⅔ cup (150 g) vegan butter, softened

½ cup (100 g) granulated sugar

1½ cups (190 g) all-purpose flour

¼ tsp salt

½ cup (85 g) vegan chocolate chips (see Tip)

Preheat the oven to 350°F (180°C). Line an 8 x 8-inch (20 x 20-cm) baking pan with parchment paper.

In a bowl with a handheld mixer or with a stand mixer, cream together the soft butter and granulated sugar until fluffy, about 2 minutes. Sift the flour and salt onto the creamed butter and sugar and mix them together. Fold in the chocolate chips and knead with your hands into a solid dough.

Press the cookie dough into the prepared baking pan.

Bake the shortbread in the oven for 25 to 30 minutes or until slightly golden brown. Poke holes in the baked shortbread cookie with a fork. Let it cool in the baking pan for 15 minutes.

Lift the cookie from the baking pan and cut it into rectangles.

Store the shortbread at room temperature in an airtight container for up to a week.

Tip: Use vegan milk chocolate chips or chopped vegan milk chocolate if you want your shortbread cookies to be sweeter.

# Berry and Fruit Lover's Cookies

Sweet as a strawberry, cozy as an apple pie, these berry and fruit lover's cookies are for you if you are craving fruity flavors. The inspiration for this chapter comes from the beautiful berries and fruits of the seasons, with each flavor captured in a cute cookie form.

To begin the chapter we're journeying toward summer with delicious Strawberries and Cream Whoopie Pies (page 59). These cake-like cookies taste like strawberry cake on a warm summer day. Our next season is fall, and cozy apple pie flavors come together in both rustic Caramel Apple Pie Cookies (page 60) and soft half-moon Apple Butter Cookies (page 63).

The cookies in this fruity chapter are classic cookies with a twist like the Fruit Jam Thumbprint Cookies with rolled oats in the dough (page 67) or jam-filled Cherry Linzer Cookies (page 68). There are also creative cookies with tropical flavors like Piña Colada Cookies (page 64), reminding me of swaying palm trees by the beach, or Strawberry Coconut Clouds (page 71), floating away in their sweet pastel-colored coating.

If it is a cheesecake flavor or citrusy zing you are craving, try the cute and not-too-sweet Raspberry Cheesecake Cookies (page 77) or the Citrus Sandwich Cookies (page 73) with a melt-in-your-mouth texture.

Have a fruity and berrylicious journey!

# Strawberries and Cream Whoopie Pies

Whoopie pies can be classified as cookies, pies, cakes or sandwiches. And indeed, these Strawberries and Cream Whoopie Pies taste and look like a combination of all of them. When making whoopie pies you need to have the right texture. The cookies need to be soft but strong enough to carry a dollop of jam and cream. This classic flavor combination reminds me of a sweet strawberry cake.

## Yield: 11 whoopie pies

1 tbsp (8 g) ground flax seeds

⅓ cup (80 g) strawberry jam

1½ cups (190 g) all-purpose flour

½ tsp baking powder

¼ tsp baking soda

¼ tsp salt

⅓ cup (75 g) vegan butter, softened

½ cup (100 g) light brown sugar

1 tsp vanilla extract

½ cup (120 g) coconut yogurt

### Filling

1 cup (250 ml) vegan whipped cream

¼ cup (50 g) vegan cream cheese

2 tbsp (30 g) granulated sugar

⅓ cup (80 g) strawberry jam

Preheat the oven to 375°F (190°C). Line two baking sheets with parchment paper.

In a small bowl, mix together the ground flax seeds and strawberry jam to form a flax "egg" and set the mixture aside. In another bowl, whisk together the flour, baking powder, baking soda and salt.

In a bowl with a handheld mixer or with a stand mixer, cream together the vegan butter, light brown sugar and vanilla extract for 2 minutes, or until fluffy. Add the flax "egg" and mix everything together with a spoon.

To the creamed butter, sugar and flax "egg" mixture, add both the flour mixture and the coconut yogurt, alternating until everything is combined together. Scoop about 1½ tablespoons (22 g) of the cookie dough and shape it into a ½-inch (1-cm)-thick cookie on the parchment paper. You can best shape the cookie with wet hands.

Bake the cookies in the oven for 10 to 14 minutes, or until they are golden brown. Remove them to a cooling rack to cool completely before assembling the whoopie pies.

In a bowl, mix together the vegan whipped cream, vegan cream cheese and granulated sugar into a thick cream. Add a dollop of cream and jam to the middle of a cookie and press another cookie gently on top. Repeat the process until all the cookies are done.

These whoopie pies are best when enjoyed the same day or the day after baking.

Store the whoopie pies in the refrigerator for up to 4 days.

# Caramel Apple Pie Cookies

These Caramel Apple Pie Cookies are like tiny apple pies with a drizzle of caramel. The cozy ingredients of these cookies—applesauce, pecans, apples and caramel together with the delicious fall spices of cinnamon, cardamom and nutmeg—form an irresistible combination. The look of these cookies is rustic, and they are easy to make. So why not try these the next time you're craving apple pie?

## Yield: 22 cookies

1 tbsp (10 g) ground flax seeds

3 tbsp (45 g) applesauce

1½ cups (190 g) all-purpose flour

1 tsp cinnamon

½ tsp ground cardamom

¼ tsp ground nutmeg

½ tsp baking powder

½ tsp baking soda

½ tsp salt

½ cup (113 g) vegan butter, softened

½ cup (100 g) granulated sugar

½ cup (100 g) brown sugar

½ cup (65 g) chopped pecans

1 cup (100 g) chopped apple

### Vegan Caramel Sauce

¼ cup (50 g) brown sugar

3 tbsp (45 ml) vegan cream such as oat-based cooking cream or coconut cream

Pinch of salt

Preheat the oven to 350°F (180°C). Line two baking sheets with parchment paper.

In a bowl, mix together the ground flax seeds with the applesauce for the flax "egg" and let it set for at least 5 minutes.

In another bowl, whisk together the flour, cinnamon, cardamom, nutmeg, baking powder, baking soda and salt.

In another bowl with a handheld mixer or with a stand mixer, cream together the vegan butter, granulated sugar and brown sugar. Stir in the flax "egg."

Mix the dry ingredients with the creamed butter, sugar and flax "egg" mixture. Fold in the chopped pecans and chopped apple and combine until the dough is firm.

Scoop about 2 tablespoons (30 g) of dough and flatten the dough into a cookie. Bake the cookies for 15 minutes.

While the cookies are baking, mix the brown sugar and vegan cream in a saucepan. Bring them to a boil and let them bubble away at low to medium heat for about 5 minutes until the caramel thickens. Add a pinch of salt. Drizzle the caramel sauce over each cookie.

Store the cookies in an airtight container at room temperature for up to 4 days, or in the refrigerator for up to a week.

# Apple Butter Cookies

One of my favorite recipes of all time is my apple butter. Although this Apple Butter Cookie recipe can be made with any applesauce or apple butter, I recommend making your own. It is not only easy but also very rewarding to have the beautiful and sweet apple aroma floating all around the house. These cute half-moon-shaped cookies are not too sweet in order to let the apple butter flavor shine through. For extra sweetness that doesn't overpower the apple butter flavor, I recommend dusting the cookies with confectioners' sugar.

## Yield: 30 cookies

1⅓ cups (170 g) all-purpose flour

⅓ cup (70 g) granulated sugar

1 tsp cinnamon

½ tsp baking powder

⅛ tsp salt

⅓ cup (75 g) vegan butter, softened

⅓ cup (80 ml) coconut cream

½ cup (120 g) apple butter or sweetened applesauce with ½–1 tsp cinnamon (see Tip)

Confectioners' sugar

**Tip:** I recommend making your own flavorful apple butter for these cookies. Chop 10 apples with their peels on into 6 pieces and cook them in the oven for 60 minutes at 300°F (150°C). Turn the heat off and cover the baking dish for 30 minutes. Remove the dish from the oven and blend the apples in a high-speed blender or food processor with maple syrup, cinnamon, cardamom, vanilla and a squeeze of lemon. Adjust the sweetness level and spices according to your taste. Store the apple butter in a clean glass jar in the refrigerator for up to 10 days.

In a bowl, whisk together the flour, granulated sugar, cinnamon, baking powder and salt. Add the vegan butter and knead with your hands into a crumbly dough. Add the coconut cream and keep kneading until you have a firm dough. Chill the dough for 15 minutes.

Preheat the oven to 390°F (200°C). Line a baking sheet with parchment paper.

On a well-floured surface, roll the dough about ¼ inch (6 mm) thick. Cut the cookies with a 2½ inch (6 cm) round cookie cutter. Place each cookie on the parchment paper.

Take about 1 teaspoon of apple butter for each cookie and dollop it on one half. Press the other half to cover the apple butter and stretch and squeeze the edges to make it stick together as a half-moon shape. Repeat the process until all the cookies are on the parchment paper.

Bake the cookies in the oven for 12 to 15 minutes, or until slightly golden brown. Let the cookies cool on the baking sheet for 15 minutes before moving them onto a cooling rack. Dust the confectioners' sugar on top of each cookie.

Store at room temperature in an airtight container for up to 4 days, or in the refrigerator for up to 6 days.

# Piña Colada Cookies

Whenever you feel like sipping a piña colada under swaying palm trees, bake these Piña Colada Cookies and pretend you're on a beach vacation. This cookie dough is made with fresh pineapple, a hint of rum and shredded coconut in the filling for an authentic piña colada taste. This cookie is a true dessert cookie thanks to its sweetness and unique flavors. You can either make sandwich cookies or enjoy each cookie like a pastry with a dollop of frosting and shredded coconut on top.

Yield: 20 cookies or 10 sandwich cookies

2 cups (250 g) all-purpose flour

½ tsp baking powder

¼ tsp baking soda

¼ tsp salt

⅔ cup (120 g) coconut sugar

½ cup (110 g) coconut oil, room temperature and scoopable

½ cup (120 ml) coconut yogurt

¾ cup (125 g) diced fresh pineapple

Filling or Frosting

1 cup (120 g) confectioners' sugar

1½ tbsp (22 ml) melted coconut oil

2 tsp (10 ml) lemon juice

1½ tsp (7.5 ml) rum

¼ cup (25 g) shredded coconut

Preheat the oven to 350°F (180°C). Line a baking sheet with parchment paper.

In a bowl, whisk together the flour, baking powder, baking soda and salt. In another bowl, mix together the coconut sugar, soft coconut oil and coconut yogurt. Combine the wet ingredients with the dry ingredients, folding gently with a spatula. Fold in the diced pineapple.

Roll about 2 tablespoons (30 g) of the dough in your hand and flatten it slightly on the parchment paper. Leave about 1 inch (2.5 cm) of space on each side of the cookie.

Bake the cookies in the oven for 10 minutes. Let the cookies cool for 15 minutes on the baking sheet before moving them onto a cooling rack.

In a bowl, mix together the confectioners' sugar, melted coconut oil, lemon juice and rum with a spoon.

If you want to make sandwich cookies, take about 2 teaspoons (15 g) of the filling and spread it on one cookie. Sprinkle the shredded coconut over the filling and press another cookie on top. To make a pastry cookie, add the frosting and shredded coconut on top of each cookie.

Store the cookies in an airtight container in the refrigerator for up to 5 days.

# Fruit Jam Thumbprint Cookies

These Fruit Jam Thumbprint Cookies are not quite like the classic version. Oats are my favorite grain, and I love to add them to baked goods to give both flavor and texture. I also added rolled oats to this classic recipe, and the oats form a lovely buttery crust together with all-purpose flour and vegan butter. Use a selection of your favorite jams for these elegant cookies to make them colorful.

## Yield: 22 cookies

1 cup (125 g) all-purpose flour

⅓ cup (30 g) rolled oats

½ tsp vanilla bean powder

½ tsp baking powder

⅛ tsp salt

½ cup (115 g) vegan butter, softened

⅓ cup (70 g) granulated sugar

⅓ cup (80 g) fruit jams such as apricot jam, orange jam, strawberry jam or raspberry jam

Preheat the oven to 350°F (180°C). Line a baking sheet with parchment paper.

In a bowl, whisk together the flour, rolled oats, vanilla bean powder, baking powder and salt.

In another bowl with a handheld mixer or with a stand mixer, cream together the vegan butter and granulated sugar. Mix the dry ingredients with the creamed butter and sugar and knead into a dough with your hands.

Take about 1 tablespoon (15 g) of the cookie dough and roll it into a ball. Flatten it on the parchment paper and gently make an indentation in the middle with your thumb. Fill the hole to the brim with jam. Repeat the process until you have filled all the cookies.

Bake the cookies in the oven for 10 to 12 minutes.

Let the cookies cool on the baking sheet for 10 minutes before moving them onto a cooling rack.

Store the cookies in an airtight container at room temperature for up to 4 days, or in the refrigerator for up to 6 days.

# Cherry Linzer Cookies

Whenever I visit my sister who lives in Germany, I buy a big heart-shaped Linzer cookie. I simply can't resist this festive, pretty cookie with a wholesome nutty flavor and sweet berry jam. The Linzer cookie, a classic Austrian cookie, is made with either ground almonds or ground hazelnuts in the cookie dough and a red currant or raspberry jam filling. Because I love both almonds and hazelnuts, I decided to make this recipe with both. And as for the jam, I recommend trying this classic recipe with cherry jam for a perfectly tart and sweet result.

## Yield: about 35 cookies

½ cup (70 g) almonds

½ cup (65 g) hazelnuts

1½ cups (190 g) all-purpose flour

1 tsp cinnamon

¼ tsp cloves

¼ tsp salt

¾ cup (170 g) vegan butter, softened

¼ cup (60 ml) maple syrup

1 cup (200 g) cherry jam

1-2 tsp (3-6 g) confectioners' sugar

Toast the almonds and hazelnuts in a dry skillet for 1 to 2 minutes on high heat. Stir every now and then so they won't burn. Remove them to a bowl or plate and let them cool for 5 minutes.

In a blender or food processor, blend the toasted almonds and hazelnuts into a flour for about 2 to 3 minutes. You should have 1⅓ cups (135 g) of nut flour. Mix the nut flour, all-purpose flour, cinnamon, cloves and salt together. Add the soft vegan butter and maple syrup and knead with your hands to get a solid firm dough. Chill the dough in the refrigerator for 30 minutes.

Preheat the oven to 350°F (180°C). Line a baking sheet with parchment paper.

Roll the dough out so that it is ⅕ inch (5 mm) thick. Make the cookies with a cookie cutter about 1½ inches (4 cm) in diameter and place them on the parchment paper close to each other. Take a small cookie cutter and take out a piece from the middle of half of the cookies. You can either bake these tiny cookies or use the dough to make more Linzer cookies.

Bake the cookies in the oven for 8 to 10 minutes, or until the cookies are slightly golden brown. Let the cookies cool for 10 minutes on the baking sheet before moving them onto a cooling rack.

Repeat the process until you have baked all the cookies.

Spread about 1½ teaspoons (6 g) of the cherry jam on a cookie and place the cookie with the tiny cookie cut out on top. Press down gently and dust the cookies with confectioners' sugar.

Store the Linzer cookies at room temperature for up to 3 days, or in the refrigerator for up to a week.

# Strawberry Coconut Clouds

These dreamy cookies are inspired by the beautiful pastel-colored forest sunsets I witnessed last summer with my daughter. Strawberries and coconut form a unique flavor match in these sweet and tender cloud cookies. Use a natural coloring such as berry powder to make the pink color, and sprinkle the clouds with your favorite vegan sprinkles. I hope these cookies will remind you of happy moments shared with loved ones too!

Yield: 12 sandwich cookies

1 ½ cups (190 g) all-purpose flour

½ cup (50 g) shredded coconut

¼ tsp salt

⅔ cup (150 g) vegan butter, softened

½ cup (60 g) confectioners' sugar

In a bowl, whisk together the flour, shredded coconut and salt.

In another bowl with a handheld mixer or with a stand mixer, cream together the vegan butter and confectioners' sugar. Mix the dry ingredients with the creamed butter and sugar and combine them into a dough with your hands. Chill the dough in the refrigerator for 30 minutes.

Preheat the oven to 350°F (180°C). Line a baking sheet with parchment paper.

Roll the dough about ⅕ inch (5 mm) thick. Cut out the cookies with a cookie cutter and place them on the parchment paper. I use a large cloud-shaped cookie cutter 3 inches (8 cm) (widest part) x 2½ inches (6 cm) (highest part). If you're using a smaller cookie cutter, you will get more cookies.

The cookies do not spread a lot, so you can keep them close to each other on the parchment paper.

Bake the cookies for 10 to 12 minutes.

Let the cookies cool on the baking sheet for 10 minutes before moving them onto a cooling rack.

(continued)

# Strawberry Coconut Clouds (Continued)

### Filling
⅓ cup (80 g) strawberry jam, room temperature

¼ cup (30 g) confectioners' sugar

2 tbsp (30 ml) coconut oil, melted

### Icing
¾ cup (90 g) confectioners' sugar

4 tsp (20 ml) lemon juice

½ tsp raspberry powder

2 tbsp (12 g) vegan sprinkles

Let the cookies cool completely before filling them.

For the filling, in a bowl, mix together the strawberry jam, confectioners' sugar and melted coconut oil.

For the icing, in another bowl, mix together the confectioners' sugar, lemon juice and raspberry powder.

Spread about 1 to 2 teaspoons (depending on the size of the cookie) of the filling on each cookie and press another cookie on top. Spread the icing on top of the top cookie and coat it with vegan sprinkles.

Store the cookies in an airtight container in the refrigerator for up to a week. The cookies and the filling will become hard when they are cold. You can take them out of the refrigerator about 30 minutes ahead of eating them to make them softer.

# Citrus Sandwich Cookies

If you are craving a cookie with a little zing, let me introduce you to the two-flavored Citrus Sandwich Cookie. The cookies are made with both lime and lemon flavors, and you will be pleasantly surprised by the perfect balance of citrusy sweetness. They are soft, and the citrus filling is creamy but firm, making these two the perfect pair for a sandwich cookie. These cookies are colored the natural way with matcha powder for the green color and turmeric powder for the bright yellow.

## Yield: 32 sandwich cookies

2 cups (250 g) all-purpose flour

½ cup (50 g) almond meal

1 cup (120 g) confectioners' sugar

¼ tsp salt

¾ cup (170 g) vegan butter, cold

1 tbsp (15 ml) lemon juice

1 tbsp (15 ml) water

½–1 tsp of lemon zest from 1 lemon

In a bowl, whisk together the flour, almond meal, confectioners' sugar and salt.

In another bowl with a handheld mixer or with a stand mixer, pulse together the dry ingredients and the cold vegan butter. Put a cover on top of the bowl to keep the flour and sugar from flying away.

Add the lemon juice, water and lemon zest and knead everything together with your hands into a dough.

Chill the dough for 30 minutes in the refrigerator.

Preheat the oven to 375°F (190°C). Line two baking sheets with parchment paper.

Divide the dough in half and roll one half with a rolling pin about ⅕ inch (5 mm) thick. Cut the cookies out with a round cookie cutter about 1¾ inches (4.5 cm) in diameter and place them on the lined baking sheet. The cookies do not spread a lot, so you can place them close to each other.

(continued)

# Citrus Sandwich Cookies (Continued)

**Filling**

⅓ cup (75 g) vegan butter, softened

1 cup (120 g) confectioners' sugar

1½ tbsp (22 ml) lemon juice

¼ tsp turmeric powder

1½ tbsp (22 ml) lime juice

¼ tsp matcha powder

Bake the cookies for 7 to 9 minutes, or until they are slightly golden on the edges. Move the cookies to a cooling rack to cool.

Repeat the process with the other half of the dough.

To make the filling, beat the soft vegan butter together with the confectioners' sugar until fluffy. Divide the cream into two bowls. To the first half, mix in the lemon juice and turmeric powder. To the second half, mix in the lime juice and matcha powder.

When the cookies have completely cooled, spread about 1 teaspoon of either lemon or lime filling between two cookies. Press them gently together. Repeat the process until all the cookies are filled.

Store the cookies in an airtight container at room temperature for up to 5 days.

The day after baking, the cookies will soften and the filling will harden a bit so that it won't spread when you bite the cookie.

# Raspberry Cheesecake Cookies

When you feel like having cheesecake but you want to make the cutest version, make these Raspberry Cheesecake Cookies! This recipe was inspired by the first cheesecake I ate in New York over ten years ago. Before that I had never paired cheesecake with raspberries, although I knew it was a classic combination. Now these two flavors come together in a mini cheesecake cookie with a creamy vegan filling made of cashews, all topped with a fresh raspberry. This cookie is not overly sweet, but you can dust each cookie with confectioners' sugar to make it sweeter.

## Yield: 14 cookies

### Filling
½ cup (70 g) cashews

3 tbsp (45 ml) lemon juice

½ tsp lemon zest or the zest of 1 lemon

3 tbsp (45 ml) water

2 tbsp (30 ml) maple syrup

### Cookies
1 cup (125 g) all-purpose flour

¼ tsp salt

⅓ cup (75 g) vegan butter, softened

3 tbsp (45 ml) maple syrup

½ tsp vanilla extract

14 fresh raspberries

1–2 tsp confectioners' sugar

**Tip:** You can also enjoy these cookies with fresh strawberries or raspberry jam or strawberry jam if you don't have raspberries.

Soak the cashews in just-boiled water for 15 minutes. Drain and rinse them well.

Preheat the oven to 350°F (180°C). Line a baking sheet with parchment paper.

In a blender, blend the soaked cashews together with the lemon juice, lemon zest, water and maple syrup until you have a smooth and creamy mixture. You might need to scrape the mixture down from the edges when blending to get everything smooth.

To make the cookies, in a bowl, whisk together the flour and salt. Add the vegan butter, maple syrup and vanilla extract and combine either with a wooden spoon, a spatula or with your hands into a smooth dough.

Take 1 tablespoon (16 g) of the dough and roll it into a ball. Flatten it on the parchment paper and shape the cookie dough into a mini pie with edges. Fill the cookie with cashew cream, about 2 teaspoons (10 ml) per cookie.

Repeat until you have all the cookies on the parchment paper. Bake the cookies in the oven for 15 minutes, or until the cashew cream is solid.

Let the cookies cool on the parchment paper for 10 minutes before moving them onto a cooling rack.

Place a fresh raspberry on each cookie and dust each cookie with confectioners' sugar.

Store the cookies in an airtight container in the refrigerator for up to 3 days.

# Cranberry Triangles

These cookies are special and they disappear fast! Cranberry Triangles are full of flavor: a hint of cinnamon, brown sugar and cranberries form a scrumptious cookie that you can't stop eating. The secret to the fudgy texture and extra sweetness of these cookies is cashew butter mixed with brown sugar. Dollops of this sugary paste are swirled into the cookie dough before baking.

### Yield: 18 triangle cookies

2 cups (250 g) all-purpose flour

1 tsp cinnamon

½ tsp baking soda

¼ tsp salt

⅔ cup (150 g) vegan butter, softened

½ cup (100 g) granulated sugar

¾ cup (150 g) light brown sugar, divided

1 cup (120 g) dried cranberries

¼ cup (60 g) cashew butter

Preheat the oven to 350°F (180°C). Line a 6½ x 10-inch (16 x 26-cm) brownie pan with parchment paper.

In a bowl, whisk together the flour, cinnamon, baking soda and salt.

In another bowl with a handheld mixer or with a stand mixer, cream together the vegan butter, granulated sugar and ½ cup (100 g) of light brown sugar until fluffy and creamy, about 2 minutes. Combine the dry ingredients and the wet ingredients with a wooden spoon or a spatula. Fold in the dried cranberries and knead with your hands until the dough is firm. In a separate bowl, mix the cashew butter and the remaining ¼ cup (50 g) of light brown sugar together to form a sugary paste.

Press the cookie dough into the baking pan. Add small dollops of the cashew butter and sugar paste evenly on top of the cookie dough. Press it slightly inside the cookie dough.

Bake the cookie in the oven for 20 to 25 minutes, or until golden brown. Let the cookie cool in the pan for 15 minutes.

Remove the cookie from the pan and cut it into triangles.

Store the cookie in an airtight container at room temperature for up to 5 days.

# Mouthwatering Cookie Bars

Cookie bars are fun and easy to make! Unlike cookies, cookie bars are just pressed in a baking tin and cut into squares or bars after cooling. My cookie bars come in all shapes and textures, both cookie-like and cake-like, with frosting and without frosting, and they are all fantastically delicious.

With flavors varying from lemon to cookie butter to rich chocolate and blueberry and yogurt, I have a treat to match all of your cravings.

If it is a totally new experience you're after, I warmly recommend starting with a classic Nordic flavor: the Runeberg Torte Bar (page 87) with its exquisite flavors of orange, cardamom and almond extract. Another Nordic classic is the Tosca cake, which is even better as a Buttery Almond Cookie Bar (page 84) with a rich texture and caramel topping.

Or maybe you are looking for a classic decadent chocolate treat? If this is the case, I recommend the Kitchen Sink Brownies (page 93), where you can dump all the leftovers from a bag of vegan marshmallows, chocolates, nuts and pretzels to make a scrumptious sweet and salty treat.

For some serious sweet cravings, I recommend the finger-licking-good Cookie Butter Bars (page 94), with a generous amount of cookie butter in both the dough and the topping, or the Chocolate Vanilla Bars (page 89), with a rich chocolate cookie coated with velvety baked cashew cream.

If you want a gluten-free treat, I have the mouthwatering Blueberry Yogurt Bars (page 102), which taste like blueberry cheesecake, or a sweet and salty combination of peanuts and berries in the Peanut Butter and Berry Jam Streusel Bars (page 101).

Two cozy flavors are also presented in this chapter: pumpkin pie–spiced Pumpkin Pie Bars (page 97) and gingerbread-spiced Gingerbread Fudge Bars, with a beautiful cranberry cream cheese frosting (page 98).

Enjoy the journey to the flavorful world of fantastic cookie bars!

# Birthday Cake Bars

These Birthday Cake Bars taste like a lemony sweet birthday cake with a melt-in-your-mouth texture and creamy frosting. These bars are liked by both children and adults, and they are not overly sweet thanks to the citrusy flavors. In addition to lemon, the dough and the frosting contain a special ingredient that makes these bars lush and soft: coconut yogurt. Vegan sprinkles, which do not spread color when baked, are a must when making these fun and pretty bars.

## Yield: 15 bars

½ cup (100 g) granulated sugar

⅓ cup (75 g) vegan butter, softened

⅓ cup (80 g) coconut yogurt

1 tsp vanilla extract

1¾ cups (225 g) all-purpose flour

⅓ cup (30 g) almond meal

½ tsp baking powder

¼ tsp baking soda

½ tsp salt

1 tsp zest of 1 small lemon

¼ cup (40 g) vegan sprinkles

### Frosting

1 cup (120 g) confectioners' sugar

2 tbsp (30 g) coconut yogurt

1 tbsp (15 ml) lemon juice

¼ cup (40 g) vegan sprinkles

Preheat the oven to 350°F (180°C). Line a 6½ x 10-inch (16 x 26-cm) brownie pan with parchment paper.

In a bowl with a handheld mixer or with a stand mixer, cream together the granulated sugar, soft vegan butter, coconut yogurt and vanilla extract until they are fluffy.

In another bowl, whisk together the flour, almond meal, baking powder, baking soda, salt and lemon zest.

Combine the wet ingredients with the dry ingredients and mix them until you have a solid dough. Fold the vegan sprinkles into the dough.

Press the dough into the bottom of the prepared pan and bake it for 20 to 25 minutes, or until the cookie feels firm. Let the cookie cool in the pan completely before spreading the frosting. In a bowl, mix together the confectioners' sugar, coconut yogurt and lemon juice. Spread the frosting on top of the cooled cookie. Decorate it with the vegan sprinkles.

Remove the cookie from the pan and let it set in the refrigerator for at least an hour before cutting it into bars.

Store the cookie bars in the refrigerator for up to 5 days.

# Buttery Almond Cookie Bars (Tosca Cake Bars)

Buttery Almond Cookie Bars, or in other words Tosca Cake Bars, are inspired by a classic Nordic recipe. Tosca cake is a sweet buttery cake with an almond caramel coating. My mother makes the best Tosca cake, and this is a modified vegan and more cookie-like version of her recipe. Try one cookie bar and be mesmerized by the beautiful buttery and caramel flavors.

## Yield: 15 bars

1 cup (125 g) all-purpose flour
¾ cup (80 g) almond meal
⅓ cup (70 g) granulated sugar
1 tsp baking powder
½ tsp ground cardamom
¼ tsp salt
⅔ cup (150 g) vegan butter, softened

### Almond Caramel
⅓ cup (80 g) vegan butter
⅓ cup (70 g) granulated sugar
1 cup (80 g) almond flakes
1 tbsp (8 g) all-purpose flour
⅛ tsp salt

Preheat the oven to 375°F (190°C). Line a 5½ x 7½-inch (14 x 19–cm) baking pan with parchment paper.

In a bowl, mix together the flour, almond meal, granulated sugar, baking powder, ground cardamom and salt. Add the soft vegan butter and knead with your hands until you have a solid dough.

Press the dough into the baking pan and bake it for 10 minutes.

To make the almond caramel, in a saucepan over low-medium heat, warm the vegan butter, granulated sugar, almond flakes, flour and salt on the stovetop, constantly stirring. Bring the ingredients to a boil and remove the pan from the heat.

Spread the almond caramel on top of the prebaked cookie. Bake it for another 15 minutes and let the cookie bars cool in the pan for 20 minutes.

Remove the cookie from the pan and cut it into squares or bars.

Store the cookie bars in an airtight container at room temperature for up to 5 days.

# Runeberg Torte Bars

I am proud to present to you one of the most classic Finnish treats. Runeberg Torte is a traditional Finnish pastry named after our national poet Johan Ludvig Runeberg. He enjoyed this unique torte for breakfast, but I recommend these sweet cookie bars as dessert. They are hearty with a lovely chewy cookie bar texture and the traditional sweet Runeberg Torte topping: sugary icing and raspberry jam. The flavor of the classic torte is exquisite and not common in cookie bars: almond extract, orange and cardamom. It is this exact flavor profile that makes these cookie bars unique and delicious.

## Yield: 18 bars

⅔ cup (150 g) vegan butter, softened

⅔ cup (145 g) light brown sugar

⅛ tsp almond extract

1 tbsp (15 ml) orange juice

1½ cups (190 g) all-purpose flour

½ cup (50 g) almond meal

¼ cup (30 g) fine bread crumbs

2 tsp (4 g) ground cardamom

½ tsp baking powder

½ tsp orange zest

¼ tsp salt

Preheat the oven to 375°F (190°C). Line a 6½ x 10-inch (16 x 26-cm) brownie pan with parchment paper.

In a bowl with a handheld mixer or with a stand mixer, cream together the vegan butter and light brown sugar until creamy and fluffy. Add the almond extract and orange juice and keep on beating. No worries if the mixture curdles because it will all come together smoothly in the dough.

In another bowl, whisk together the flour, almond meal, bread crumbs, cardamom, baking powder, orange zest and salt.

Combine the dry ingredients with the wet ingredients by folding them gently with a wooden spoon or spatula. Knead the dough with your hands until it is solid and firm.

(continued)

# Runeberg Torte Bars (Continued)

**Icing**
1 cup (120 g) confectioners' sugar
2-3 tbsp (30-45 ml) orange juice
½ cup (120 g) raspberry jam

Press the dough evenly into a prepared baking pan. Bake it in the oven for 15 to 20 minutes or until golden brown and firm.

Let the cookie cool in the pan for 15 minutes before removing it, then allow it to cool completely before spreading the icing and jam on top.

In a bowl, mix the confectioners' sugar with the orange juice until smooth.

With a spoon, make a stripe of the icing on top of the cookie. Then make another stripe with the raspberry jam. Continue alternating with the icing and the jam until you have covered the whole cookie.

Once the icing has firmed up, you can cut the cookie into bars or squares. For best—less messy—results, keep the cookie in the refrigerator for 30 minutes before cutting.

Store the cookie bars in an airtight container in the refrigerator for up to a week.

# Chocolate Vanilla Bars

A classic flavor combination and a perfect chewy and soft texture come together in these delicious Chocolate Vanilla Bars. The cookie bars consist of a thick dark chocolate cookie layer and a melt-in-your-mouth velvety baked vanilla cream layer made from cashews. This flavor is classic for a reason—these two together are both familiar and festive. To make these cookie bars you need a high-speed blender or food processor to blend the vanilla layer as smooth as possible.

## Yield: 16-20 bars

**Vanilla Layer**

1 cup (150 g) cashews, unsalted and unroasted

¼ cup (50 g) granulated sugar

1 tsp vanilla extract

⅓ cup (80 ml) plant-based milk such as oat milk

**Chocolate Layer**

⅓ cup (55 g) vegan dark chocolate chips or chunks

½ cup (115 g) vegan butter, softened

½ cup (100 g) granulated sugar

½ tsp vanilla extract

Soak the cashews in a bowl filled with hot water for about 15 minutes. Drain them and rinse them well.

Preheat the oven to 375°F (190°C). Line an 8 x 8-inch (20 x 20-cm) baking pan with parchment paper.

Blend the cashews with the granulated sugar, vanilla extract and plant-based milk in a high-speed blender for 1 to 3 minutes, or until you have a velvety smooth cream. Set it aside.

Melt the dark chocolate chips or chunks on the stovetop by first filling a saucepan with about 1 inch (2.5 cm) of water. Place the chocolate in a heatproof bowl on top of the saucepan. Make sure the bowl is not touching the water and that no water gets in the chocolate bowl (or else the chocolate will become lumpy). Warm the chocolate on medium heat, stirring for about 2 minutes, or until the chocolate is smooth. Set the melted chocolate aside to cool for a few minutes.

In a bowl with a handheld mixer or with a stand mixer, cream together the soft butter, granulated sugar and vanilla extract until creamy. Fold in the melted chocolate.

(continued)

# Chocolate Vanilla Bars (Continued)

1½ cups (155 g) all-purpose flour

½ tsp baking powder

¼ tsp baking soda

¼ tsp salt

¼ cup (40 g) vegan dark chocolate chips or small pieces of chocolate

In another bowl, whisk the flour, baking powder, baking soda and salt together. Combine the dry ingredients with the wet ingredients and knead gently with your hand to get a firm dough. Fold in the dark chocolate chips.

Press the cookie dough into the prepared baking pan.

Spread the vanilla cashew cream on top of the chocolate cookie dough.

Bake it in the oven for 25 to 30 minutes until the top layer has a mild golden color.

Let it cool in the pan for 15 minutes. Remove the cookie from the pan and cut it into squares or bars.

If you store the cookie in the refrigerator for an hour or more, it is easier to cut into squares or bars.

Store the cookie bars in the refrigerator in an airtight container for up to 6 days.

# Kitchen Sink Brownies

What I love about these "everything but the kitchen sink" brownies is that each time I make them, they taste different, and each time they taste delicious. They are soft straight from the oven but are fudgy like candy bars after a night in the refrigerator. Either way, these brownies are a perfect treat to satisfy chocolate cravings, especially if your "everything but the kitchen sink" includes lots of extra chocolate. You can also use anything you love: nuts and pretzels, vegan marshmallows or vegan cookies.

## Yield: 16–20 bars

½ cup (115 g) vegan butter

1 cup (95 g) almond meal

½ cup (65 g) all-purpose flour or all-purpose gluten-free flour

½ cup (45 g) cocoa powder

½ cup (100 g) granulated sugar

½ tsp baking soda

¼ tsp salt

½ cup (120 ml) plant-based milk such as oat milk

1 cup (170 g) vegan chocolate chips or chocolate chunks, divided

1 cup (about 100–150 g) mix-ins such as vegan white or milk chocolate chunks, vegan marshmallows, vegan chocolate shell candies, pieces of vegan cookies or pretzels, chopped walnuts or pecans

Preheat the oven to 350°F (180°C). Line an 8 x 8-inch (20 x 20-cm) baking pan with parchment paper so that the brownies are easier to lift from the pan.

Melt the vegan butter in a bowl in the microwave or on the stovetop over low-medium heat in a saucepan.

In a bowl, combine the almond meal, flour, cocoa powder, granulated sugar, baking soda and salt. Add the melted butter and plant-based milk and fold the batter gently. Add the vegan chocolate chips or chocolate chunks and 1 cup (100 to 150 g) of mix-ins to the brownie batter and fold everything together gently. You can also leave some of the mix-ins as a decoration on top of the brownie.

Pour the batter into the prepared baking pan. Bake it on the middle rack of the oven for 35 to 40 minutes, or until the brownie is still soft but not raw. You can check this with a toothpick: If a lot of raw batter sticks to the toothpick, keep baking it a few minutes at a time until it is ready and the toothpick comes out clean. The brownie will be crumbly straight from the oven, but it will firm up once cooled.

Let the brownie cool completely in the pan before removing it. Once removed from the pan, let it cool completely in the refrigerator for an hour or overnight before cutting it into pieces.

Store the brownies in the refrigerator for up to a week.

# Cookie Butter Bars

If you can resist eating all the cookie butter straight from the jar, I urge you to bake these scrumptious treats that have a wonderful chewy texture. Cookie Butter Bars are a delight to anyone who loves cookie butter, and even if you don't, these cookies might make you change your mind. Cookie butter is a flavored spread made from Speculoos cookies. When you combine cookie butter and chocolate, you get an even more mind-blowing sweet experience. To adjust the level of sweetness, use either sweet vegan milk chocolate or a not-so-sweet darker (such as 80%) chocolate.

### Yield: 8 large bars or 16 small bars

¼ cup (60 g) vegan butter, softened

⅓ cup (70 g) light brown sugar

3 tbsp (45 ml) aquafaba (see Tips)

1 cup (125 g) all-purpose flour

½ tsp baking powder

¼ tsp salt

½ cup (130 g) cookie butter or Speculoos spread (see Tips)

#### Chocolate Layer
¾ cup (130 g) vegan milk chocolate

¼ cup (65 g) cookie butter or Speculoos spread

**Tips:** Aquafaba is the liquid from a can of chickpeas or white beans. It can be used as a vegan "egg." Three tablespoons (45 ml) of aquafaba can be used in place of one egg.

Be sure to double check that the brand of cookie butter you use is vegan. Lotus Biscoff cookie butter and Trader Joe's Speculoos cookie butter are both vegan.

Preheat the oven to 350°F (180°C). Line an 8 x 4-inch (21 x 11-cm) baking pan with parchment paper.

In a bowl with a handheld mixer or with a stand mixer, cream together the vegan butter and light brown sugar for 2 minutes, or until creamy and fluffy. Add the aquafaba and keep beating for another minute until everything is combined.

In another bowl, whisk together the flour, baking powder and salt.

Combine the dry ingredients with the wet ingredients and mix them together with a wooden spoon or spatula. Fold in the cookie butter and press the cookie dough into the prepared baking pan.

Bake it in the oven for 15 minutes. Let the cookie cool in the pan for 15 minutes.

Melt the vegan milk chocolate on the stovetop by first filling a saucepan with about 1 inch (2.5 cm) of water. Place the chocolate in a heatproof bowl on top of the saucepan. Make sure the bowl is not touching the water and that no water gets in the chocolate bowl (or else the chocolate will become lumpy). Warm the chocolate on medium heat, stirring for about 2 minutes, or until the chocolate is smooth. Add the cookie butter to the melted chocolate and mix it with a spoon until the mixture is smooth. Spread the chocolate layer on top of the cookie layer.

Let it cool in the freezer for 15 to 30 minutes before cutting it into 8 large bars or 16 small bars.

Store it in the refrigerator in an airtight container for up to 8 days or in the freezer for up to 1 month.

# Pumpkin Pie Bars

Pumpkin pie in cookie bar form is a spicy delicious treat. It is especially suitable when you are craving the cozy spices of fall and winter: cinnamon, cardamom, cloves and nutmeg. With a pecan and oat cookie crust, a soft and sweet pumpkin-date layer and a creamy vegan whipped cream topping, this bar is a lovely dessert for any occasion. You need an immersion blender or food processor to make the pumpkin layer as smooth as possible.

## Yield: 16-20 bars

⅓ cup (35 g) pecans
¾ cup (70 g) rolled oats
⅔ cup (85 g) all-purpose flour
1 tsp cinnamon
½ tsp ground cardamom
⅛ tsp cloves
⅛ tsp nutmeg
¼ tsp salt
⅓ cup (75 g) vegan butter, softened
¼ cup (60 ml) maple syrup

### Pumpkin Layer
⅔ cup (160 g) pumpkin purée
½ cup (100 g) pitted dates such as medjool dates
½ tsp cinnamon
¼ tsp ground cardamom
Pinch of salt

### Top Layer
1½ cups (360 ml) vegan whipped cream

Preheat the oven to 375°F (190°C). Line an 8 x 8-inch (20 x 20-cm) baking pan with parchment paper.

In a blender or food processor, blend the pecans and rolled oats into a flour for about 2 minutes. Mix the pecan and oat flour mixture with the all-purpose flour, cinnamon, cardamom, cloves, nutmeg and salt.

Add the vegan butter and maple syrup and combine into a cookie dough. If the dough feels too dry, add water ½ tablespoon (7.5 ml) at a time.

Press the dough into the prepared baking pan. Prebake the cookie for 10 minutes.

In a food processor or with an immersion blender, blend the pumpkin purée, pitted dates, cinnamon, cardamom and salt until smooth. Spread the pumpkin layer on top of the cookie dough layer.

Bake it in the oven for 10 minutes. Let it cool in the pan for 30 minutes before moving it onto a cooling rack.

When the pumpkin layer has completely cooled, spread the vegan whipped cream evenly on top. Store the cookie in the refrigerator for 30 to 60 minutes before cutting it into bars or squares.

Store the cookie bars in the refrigerator in an airtight container for up to 5 days (depending on the brand of vegan whipped cream used, the storing time might be less than 5 days due to the expiration date).

# Gingerbread Fudge Bars

Imagine all the delicious festive gingerbread flavors brought together in the most chewy and fudgy bar! These Gingerbread Fudge Bars have a delicious cranberry-cream cheese frosting that brings a lovely tart balance to the sweet gingerbread flavors. Another balancing ingredient is the salty brown miso paste in the cookie dough to bring a little mouthwatering umami flavor. Although the look and flavor of these bars are festive, they taste amazing all year 'round.

### Yield: 16-20 bars

1 cup (200 g) pitted dates such as medjool dates

¾ cup (170 g) vegan butter

½ cup (110 g) brown sugar

2 tsp (10 ml) brown rice miso paste (see Tip)

1½ cups (190 g) all-purpose flour

3 tsp (7.5 g) cinnamon

2 tsp (10 g) grated fresh ginger or 1 tsp ground ginger

1 tsp ground cardamom

½ tsp baking soda

⅛ tsp salt

### Frosting

⅔ cup (160 ml) vegan whipped cream

⅓ cup (80 g) vegan cream cheese

⅓ cup (90 g) sweetened cranberry jam

⅓ cup (50 g) cranberries

Preheat the oven to 350°F (180°C). Line an 8 x 8-inch (20 x 20-cm) baking pan with parchment paper.

In a saucepan on the stovetop over medium heat, warm the dates, vegan butter and brown sugar, constantly stirring until the dates are mostly dissolved. Add the miso paste and blend the mixture with an immersion blender until everything is smooth. Let the mixture cool for 5 minutes.

In a bowl, whisk together the flour, cinnamon, ginger, cardamom, baking soda and salt.

Combine the wet ingredients with the dry ingredients and mix with a wooden spoon, spatula or with your hands until the cookie dough is smooth.

Press the dough evenly into the prepared baking pan and bake it for 15 minutes. Let the cookie cool in the pan completely before removing it.

In a bowl, mix together the vegan whipped cream, vegan cream cheese and sweetened cranberry jam with a spoon until they are smooth. Spread the frosting on top of the gingerbread and cut it into squares or bars. Decorate the bars with cranberries.

Store the bars in an airtight container in the refrigerator for up to 6 days.

Tip: You can also make these bars without miso paste. Just add ¼ teaspoon more salt to balance the flavors.

# Peanut Butter and Berry Jam Streusel Bars

The combination of a buttery oat crust, sweet berry jam and salted peanut streusel is irresistible. These easy-to-make cookie bars are like eating a crunchy peanut butter and jam toast with salted peanuts sprinkled on top. The secret to the tastiness of these gluten-free bars is the perfect balance of sweet berry jam and salted peanuts.

Yield: 16 bars

⅔ cup (150 g) vegan butter

2½ cups (250 g) gluten-free oat flour

⅔ cup (150 g) light brown sugar

¼ tsp salt

⅓ cup (90 g) smooth peanut butter

⅔ cup (160 g) raspberry jam

½ cup (70 g) salted and roasted peanuts, either whole or chopped

Preheat the oven to 350°F (180°C). Line an 8 x 8-inch (20 x 20-cm) baking pan with parchment paper.

Melt the vegan butter in a bowl in the microwave or on the stovetop over low-medium heat in a pan.

In a bowl, whisk together the oat flour, light brown sugar and salt. Add the melted butter and peanut butter and combine into a solid dough.

Press half of the dough into the baking pan. Spread the raspberry jam evenly on top.

Mix the rest of the dough with the salted peanuts. Sprinkle the crumbly dough evenly on top of the raspberry jam.

Bake it in the oven for 30 to 35 minutes, or until the bottom layer is not raw. You can test this after 30 minutes by cutting a small piece of the bar and checking the layers. If the edges are still raw, the middle part will be raw too, so continue baking for about 5 minutes. The cookie bars will be crumbly straight from the oven, but they will firm up when they cool down.

Let the cookie bars cool completely in the pan, for about 30 minutes, before removing them.

Cut the cookie into bars or squares once it is completely cooled and easier to cut.

Store it in the refrigerator in an airtight container for up to a week.

Tip: Gluten-free oat flour is easy to make at home! Just use certified gluten-free rolled oats and blend them in a food processor or high-speed blender until you have a flour consistency. From 1 cup (90 g) of rolled oats you get about ¾ cup (90 g) of oat flour.

# Blueberry Yogurt Bars

Blueberry Yogurt Bars are like a lighter version of blueberry cheesecake with a similar tangy cheesecake layer made from dairy-free yogurt. Use a soy-based yogurt and cornstarch to ensure the yogurt layer firms up in the oven. The gluten-free crust is made of oat flour and almond meal, an all-time favorite flour combination when baking gluten-free. Oats, blueberries and yogurt together remind me of a traditional Finnish blueberry pie with a yogurt-like filling. I must admit I much prefer this delicious cookie bar version.

### Yield: 16 bars

1½ cups (135 g) gluten-free rolled oats

1 cup (100 g) almond meal

1 tbsp (8 g) cornstarch

1 tsp cinnamon

¼ tsp salt

½ cup (115 g) vegan butter, softened

⅓ cup (70 g) granulated sugar

¼ cup (55 g) brown sugar

### Blueberry Yogurt Layer
⅔ cup (160 ml) soy yogurt (natural or vanilla flavored)

2 tbsp (30 g) granulated sugar

2 tbsp (15 g) cornstarch

½ tsp vanilla extract

⅔ cup (100 g) blueberries (fresh or frozen)

Preheat the oven to 375°F (190°C). Line an 8 x 8-inch (20 x 20-cm) baking pan with parchment paper.

In a food processor or blender, blend the rolled oats into a flour. In a bowl, combine the oat flour with the almond meal, cornstarch, cinnamon and salt.

In a bowl with a handheld mixer or with a stand mixer, cream together the vegan butter and sugars for 2 minutes, or until creamy and fluffy.

Combine the dry ingredients with the wet ingredients and mix them together with a spoon.

Press the dough into the prepared baking pan. Bake it in the oven for 15 minutes.

In a bowl, mix together the soy yogurt with the granulated sugar, cornstarch and vanilla extract.

Spread the yogurt layer on top of the prebaked cookie layer. Sprinkle blueberries evenly on top.

Bake it in the oven for another 20 to 25 minutes, or until the yogurt and berry layer is not wobbly anymore. The layer will become more solid when the cookie is stored in the refrigerator.

Store the cookie in the refrigerator for an hour or even overnight before cutting it into bars or squares.

Store the cookie bars or squares in an airtight container in the refrigerator for up to 5 days.

# Millionaire's Tahini Caramel Cookie Bars

These Tahini Caramel Cookie Bars are my version of the famous millionaire's shortbread: a buttery crust with a gooey caramel layer and a generous coating of chocolate on top. Adding tahini to both the crust and the caramel brings this cookie bar to an exceptionally tasty level. To make these bars gluten-free I use flour made of certified gluten-free rolled oats. Use vegan milk chocolate for a sweeter flavor experience.

### Yield: 16-20 bars

2 cups (180 g) gluten-free rolled oats

¼ tsp salt

⅓ cup (80 ml) maple syrup

3 tbsp (40 g) coconut oil, room temperature and scoopable

1 tbsp (15 g) smooth tahini, hulled seed

### Caramel Layer
¼ cup (65 g) smooth tahini, hulled seed

¼ cup (60 ml) maple syrup

3 tbsp (45 g) light brown sugar

2 tbsp (27 g) coconut oil, room temperature and scoopable

Pinch of salt

### Chocolate Layer
⅔ cup (115 g) vegan chocolate chips

1½ tsp (7 g) coconut oil, room temperature and scoopable

Preheat the oven to 375°F (190°C). Line an 8 x 8-inch (20 x 20-cm) baking pan with parchment paper.

In a blender or food processor, blend the rolled oats into a flour for about 1 to 2 minutes. Combine the oat flour with the salt. Add the maple syrup, coconut oil and tahini and mix it with a wooden spoon or spatula until you have a firm dough.

Press the dough into the prepared baking pan. Bake it for 8 to 10 minutes.

To make the caramel layer, warm the tahini, maple syrup and light brown sugar in a saucepan on the stovetop over medium heat. Stir constantly for a minute so the mixture doesn't burn. Remove from the heat and mix in the coconut oil and salt.

To make the chocolate layer, melt the chocolate and coconut oil on the stovetop by first filling a saucepan with about 1 inch (2.5 cm) of water. Place the chocolate and coconut oil in a heatproof bowl on top of the saucepan. Make sure the bowl is not touching the water and that no water gets in the chocolate bowl (or else the chocolate will become lumpy). Warm the mixture on medium heat, stirring for about 2 minutes, or until the chocolate is smooth.

Spread the caramel layer on top of the oat cookie dough. Pour the melted chocolate layer on top and spread it evenly.

Let the cookie bars cool in the refrigerator for at least an hour or in the freezer for about 30 minutes. Cut them into bars or squares with a sharp knife for best results.

Store the cookie bars in the refrigerator in an airtight container for up to 7 days, or in the freezer for up to 2 months.

# Flavorful Snack Cookies

Cookie lovers' favorite snack is a cookie! Snack cookies are more wholesome than regular cookies and usually loaded with fiber, protein and good fats. They are satisfying and filling–just like a snack should be!

They are also less sweet than regular cookies and use dates, bananas, maple syrup or coconut sugar as a sweetener. You can have them as a snack or even as a healthier dessert.

When you're craving a quick snack, why not try easy-to-make blender cookies? Cranberry Date Cookies (page 109) are sweetened with just dates, and their chocolatey version, the Chocolate Coconut Cookies (page 110), are sweetened with dark chocolate and dates with a lovely flavor from toasted coconut flakes.

If you like bananas, I have two delicious snack recipes for you: a simple and wholesome Banana Coconut Cookie (page 113) and the softest Banana Bread Cookie (page 114), which tastes exactly like banana bread and is best enjoyed warm.

You can also make your favorite granola into a crunchy and crispy cookie. That's what I did with my Crispy Tahini Granola Cookies (page 117) based on my popular tahini granola recipe. This cookie is amazing not only because of the beautiful nutty tahini flavor but also because the cookie can be stored for weeks, just like granola.

Snack cookies can also be savory! Think of a beautiful platter with vegan cheese and fruits. What is missing? Of course, a savory vegan cookie flavored with herbs like the Thyme Parmesan Cookies (page 122) or Savory Pizza Cookies (page 125).

Welcome to the wonderful world of healthy and flavorful snack cookies!

# Cranberry Date Cookies

When it's a wholesome and quick-to-make cookie you're after, I have the perfect healthy recipe for you: Cranberry Date Cookies. The cookie dough is made in a blender or food processor by blending all of the ingredients together. Then you shape this dough into ten small cookies and bake them in the oven. This recipe is inspired by the first cookie I baked for my little one when he was one year old (without the salt and the icing). I used black currants to make this at the time, but with cranberries you get a lovely tart twist to the flavor. The beautifully pink sugar icing is optional but recommended if you want a sweeter snack cookie.

½ cup (45 g) gluten-free rolled oats

⅓ cup (40 g) pecans or walnuts or a mixture of both

⅓ cup (about 50 g) fresh or frozen cranberries

⅓ cup (about 80 g) pitted dates such as medjool dates, plus more as needed

1 tbsp (14 g) coconut oil, room temperature and scoopable

½ tsp cinnamon

⅛ tsp salt

### Icing
½ cup (60 g) confectioners' sugar

1 tbsp (15 ml) cranberry juice

¼ tsp raspberry powder (optional)

Preheat the oven to 375°F (190°C). Line a baking sheet with parchment paper.

In a high-speed blender or food processor, blend the oats, pecans, cranberries, pitted dates, coconut oil, cinnamon and salt until you have a coarse dough that sticks together well. Add more pitted dates, half a date (if using medjool dates) or one date (if using smaller dates) at a time if the cookie dough is too crumbly.

Take about 1½ tablespoons (22 g) of the cookie dough and roll it into a ball. Flatten the ball on the parchment paper into a ⅖-inch (1-cm)-thick cookie with a diameter of 1⅗ inches (4 cm).

Bake the cookies in the oven for 15 minutes. Let the cookies cool on the baking sheet for 15 minutes before moving them onto a cooling rack.

In a bowl, mix together the confectioners' sugar, cranberry juice and raspberry powder, if using. Spread the icing on top of the cookies.

Store the cookies in an airtight container in the refrigerator for up to 5 days, or in the freezer for up to 2 months.

Tip: Try this cookie with blueberries, red or black currants or blackberries.

# Chocolate Coconut Cookies

These simple but rich Chocolate Coconut Cookies are gluten-free and wholesome with just dates and dark chocolate as sweeteners. A lovely flavor note comes from the toasted coconut flakes. The cookie dough is easy to make in a blender. These cookies are also perfect as a healthy dessert option.

### Yield: 10 small cookies

½ cup (45 g) gluten-free rolled oats

⅓ cup (30 g) toasted coconut flakes

⅓ cup (55 g) vegan dark chocolate

⅓ cup (about 80 g) pitted dates such as medjool dates, plus more as needed

2 tbsp (27 g) coconut oil, room temperature and scoopable

⅛ tsp salt

Preheat the oven to 375°F (190°C). Line a baking sheet with parchment paper.

In a high-speed blender or food processor, blend the oats, coconut flakes, dark chocolate, pitted dates, coconut oil and salt until you have a coarse dough that sticks together well. Add half a pitted date (if using medjool dates) or one pitted date (if using smaller dates) at a time if the cookie dough is too crumbly.

Take about 1½ tablespoons (23 g) of the cookie dough and roll it into a ball. Flatten the ball on the parchment paper into a ⅖-inch (1-cm)-thick cookie with a diameter of 2 inches (5 cm).

Bake the cookies in the oven for 5 minutes.

Let the cookies cool on the baking sheet for 15 minutes. Carefully move them to a cooling rack.

Store the cookies in an airtight container in the refrigerator for up to 5 days, or in the freezer for up to 2 months.

# Banana Coconut Cookies

I created this recipe originally as a healthy and wholesome dessert for me and my children. Nowadays this is more of a quick sweet snack enjoyed on a platter with fruits and nuts. It takes about 15 minutes to make these delicious cookies, and you can get creative with the ingredients by swapping the almond or coconut butter with other nut and seed butters. Also the coconut sugar is optional, but it gives lovely caramel notes to the otherwise naturally sweetened cookies.

### Yield: 10 cookies

Heaping ⅓ cup (100 g) mashed banana (about 1 medium-sized banana)

1 cup (100 g) almond meal

½ cup (50 g) shredded coconut

2 tbsp (30 ml) coconut butter, melted

1 tbsp (15 ml) coconut oil, melted

1 tbsp (15 g) almond butter

1 tbsp (11 g) coconut sugar

½ tsp cinnamon

⅛ tsp salt

Preheat the oven to 375°F (190°C). Line a baking sheet with parchment paper.

In a bowl, mix together the mashed banana, almond meal, shredded coconut, coconut butter, coconut oil, almond butter, coconut sugar, cinnamon and salt with a spoon.

Take about 1 to 1½ tablespoons (30 g) of the cookie dough and roll it into a ball. Flatten the ball on the parchment paper into a ⅖-inch (1-cm)-thick cookie.

Bake the cookies in the oven for 10 minutes. Let them cool on the baking sheet for 15 minutes. Carefully move the cookies onto a cooling rack.

Store the cookies in an airtight container in the refrigerator for up to 3 days, or in the freezer for up to a month.

# Banana Bread Cookies

Lots of banana breads have been baked lately, but have you ever made the more simple and quick version of banana bread—Banana Bread Cookies? These naturally gluten-free cookies taste best when eaten warm, just like banana bread. They have a mild banana flavor and they are deliciously soft and cozy.

## Yield: 16 cookies

½ cup (50 g) gluten-free oat flour

½ cup (45 g) gluten-free rolled oats

1 tsp cinnamon

¼ tsp baking soda

¼ tsp salt

¼ cup (60 ml) maple syrup

¼ cup (60 g) coconut yogurt

2 tbsp (26 g) coconut oil, room temperature and scoopable

⅓ cup (80 g) mashed banana (about 1 small banana or half of a large banana)

Preheat the oven to 350°F (180°C). Line a baking sheet with parchment paper.

In a bowl, whisk together the oat flour, rolled oats, cinnamon, baking soda and salt. Add the maple syrup, coconut yogurt, coconut oil and mashed banana and mix everything together.

Scoop about 1½ tablespoons (19 g) per cookie and place it on the parchment paper. The cookies don't spread a lot, so you can place all the cookies on one baking sheet.

Bake the cookies for 12 to 14 minutes, or until they turn golden brown. Let the cookies cool on the baking sheet for 15 minutes.

The cookies are very soft straight from the oven.

Store the cookies in the refrigerator for up to 3 days. The cookies are best when slightly warm, so you can warm them up in the microwave for 15 seconds.

# Crispy Tahini Granola Cookies

When you love granola so much you want to eat it for breakfast and as a snack, why not make these gluten-free Crispy Tahini Granola Cookies? This cookie recipe is based on my favorite tahini granola recipe. With a lovely and warm nutty flavor from the tahini and nuts, and dates as a sweetener, this cookie is very wholesome and filling. The method of making these cookies is similar to making granola, but instead of spreading all the ingredients on a baking sheet, you press them into tight balls and flatten them into thin cookies. The cookies become crispy when baked and they get crispier when cooled.

## Yield: 30 cookies

1 cup (200 g) pitted medjool dates

⅓ cup (90 g) smooth tahini, hulled seed

¼ cup (55 g) coconut oil, room temperature and scoopable

1 tsp vanilla extract

2 cups (about 250–280 g) selection of chopped nuts and seeds such as cashews, almonds, walnuts, pecans, sunflower and pumpkin seeds

1½ cups (135 g) gluten-free rolled oats

3 tbsp (30 g) chia seeds

1 tsp cardamom

¼ tsp salt

4 tbsp (60 ml) maple syrup

Preheat the oven to 300°F (150°C). Line a baking sheet with parchment paper.

In a blender or food processor, blend the dates, tahini, coconut oil and vanilla extract into a smooth caramel paste.

In a bowl, mix together the chopped nuts, rolled oats, chia seeds, cardamom and salt.

Combine the date caramel paste with the dry ingredients and knead with your hands into a dough. Add the maple syrup and keep on kneading until you have a dough that is easy to shape.

Take about 1½ tablespoons (26 g) of the dough and roll it into a ball. Flatten the ball on the parchment paper into a ⅖-inch (1-cm) cookie with a diameter of 2½ inches (6 cm). If the cookie dough feels too sticky, use wet hands to shape the cookie.

Bake the cookies in the oven for 20 to 25 minutes, or until they are a bit crispy. Let them cool on the baking sheet for another 30 minutes before moving them onto a cooling rack.

Store the cookies in an airtight container at room temperature for up to a month.

*Tip:* You can also make this recipe as a granola or granola clusters. Instead of rolling each cookie into a ball and flattening it on the baking sheet, you can flatten the whole dough on the baking sheet. Bake it in the oven for about 25 to 30 minutes, or until the granola feels dry. Let the granola cool on the baking sheet for 30 minutes before breaking it into clusters.

# Masala Chai Graham Cookies

Masala Chai Graham Cookies are sweeter than the average snack cookie. The cozy and warming flavors remind me of gingerbread cookies. They are sweetened with coconut sugar and maple syrup for a lovely caramel flavor. These cookies are made from whole wheat flour and oat bran for a wholesome texture. Grab two or three cookies and enjoy them with a cup of warm chai or coffee.

## Yield: 32 cookies

½ cup (115 g) vegan butter

⅔ cup (110 g) coconut sugar

1½ cups (180 g) whole wheat flour or graham flour

⅓ cup (45 g) oat bran

½ tsp baking powder

¼ tsp salt

2 tsp (5 g) cinnamon

1 tsp cardamom

¼ tsp ginger

⅛ tsp cloves

⅛ tsp nutmeg

2 tbsp (30 ml) maple syrup

Preheat the oven to 350°F (180°C). Line two baking sheets with parchment paper.

In a bowl with a handheld mixer or with a stand mixer, cream together the vegan butter and coconut sugar for 2 minutes, or until fluffy and creamy.

In another bowl, whisk together the flour, oat bran, baking powder, salt, cinnamon, cardamom, ginger, cloves and nutmeg. Combine the dry ingredients with the creamed butter and sugar. Add the maple syrup and combine everything into a dough.

Roll the dough on a floured surface until it is about ⅕ inch (5 mm) thick. Cut out the cookies with a cookie cutter and place them on the baking sheet about 1 inch (2.5 cm) from each other.

Bake the sheets one at a time for 8 minutes. Let the cookies cool for 15 minutes and move them to a cooling rack.

The cookies will become crispier and harder after cooling completely.

Store the cookies at room temperature in an airtight container for up to 1 week.

# Savory Oat Cookies

Savory Oat Cookies with vegan shredded cheese are my version of a childhood snack I used to bake often myself. My mom taught me to make bread rolls with cheese, and this is the simple cookie version. Depending on the salt level of the vegan cheese brand, you might not need to add any extra salt to the cookie. Also the texture of the cookie might be different than pictured here depending on whether the vegan cheese melts properly when baked or not.

### Yield: 24 cookies

1 tbsp (8 g) ground flax seeds

2½ tbsp (38 ml) water

1½ cups (135 g) rolled oats

½ cup (60 g) all-purpose flour

½ tsp baking powder

¼ tsp salt

⅔ cup (150 g) vegan butter, softened

⅔ cup (75 g) + 2 tbsp (14 g) shredded vegan cheese

Preheat the oven to 350°F (180°C). Line two baking sheets with parchment paper.

In a small bowl, mix the ground flax seeds and water to create a vegan "egg." In another bowl, combine the rolled oats, flour, baking powder and salt. Add the flax "egg," vegan butter and ⅔ cup (75 g) of shredded vegan cheese and mix everything into a solid dough.

Scoop about 1½ tablespoons (22 g) of the cookie dough and roll it into a ball. Flatten the ball on the parchment paper into about a ½-inch (1-cm) cookie. Sprinkle the remaining 2 tablespoons (14 g) of shredded vegan cheese on top of each cookie.

Bake the cookies in the oven for 15 to 18 minutes, or until the cookies are slightly golden.

Let the cookies cool on the baking sheet for 15 minutes before moving them onto a cooling rack.

Store the cookies in an airtight container at room temperature for about 5 days, or in the refrigerator for up to 8 days.

# Thyme Parmesan Cookies

Savory cookies are a delicious alternative to sweet snacks. The base flavors of these cookies are thyme and vegan parmesan made from toasted sunflower seeds and nutritional yeast. This is the parmesan I make most often, and I recommend you try it with pasta too! Thyme is one of my favorite herbs, and it makes a lovely combination with the salty vegan parmesan. Enjoy these cookies as part of a snack platter or just as they are. This cookie dough makes a great savory tart crust too.

## Yield: 20 cookies

1 tbsp (8 g) ground flax seeds

2½ tbsp (38 ml) plant-based milk such as oat milk

½ cup (70 g) sunflower seeds

5 tbsp (25 g) nutritional yeast

½ tsp onion powder

¼ tsp garlic powder

¼ tsp salt

1 cup (125 g) all-purpose flour

2 tsp (2 g) dried thyme, divided

½ cup (115 g) vegan butter, softened

Preheat the oven to 350°F (180°C). Line an 8 x 8-inch (20 x 20-cm) baking pan with parchment paper.

In a bowl, mix together the ground flax seeds and plant-based milk to create a vegan "egg."

Toast the sunflower seeds in a dry pan over high heat for a minute or two, stirring occasionally. Let them cool for a few minutes in a bowl or a plate.

In a blender or food processor, blend the toasted sunflower seeds with the nutritional yeast, onion powder, garlic powder and salt until you have a coarse flour-like texture.

Mix the vegan "parmesan" flour with the all-purpose flour and 1 teaspoon of dried thyme.

Add the soft vegan butter and flax "egg" and knead gently into a dough.

Press the dough into the prepared baking pan and sprinkle 1 teaspoon of dried thyme evenly on top. Bake it in the oven for 18 to 20 minutes.

Let the cookie cool in the pan for 20 minutes before removing it.

Cut the cookie into squares or bars when it has cooled completely.

Store the cookies in an airtight container at room temperature for up to 6 days, or in the refrigerator for up to 10 days.

# Savory Pizza Cookies

There's no need to buy crackers from the grocery store anymore—these Savory Pizza Cookies are perfect with any vegan cheese and are a great spicy addition to your vegan cheese platter. The cookies are made with a simple pizza-like dough with just flour, water and olive oil as the main ingredients. The spice of the cookie is tomato purée, which together with the sesame seeds, dried herbs and the flakes of salt make for an astoundingly pizza-flavored snack.

## Yield: 30-35 cookies

1½ cups (190 g) all-purpose flour
1 tsp dried thyme
½ tsp salt
3 tbsp (45 ml) tomato purée
3½ tbsp (50 ml) water
5 tbsp (75 ml) olive oil

### Topping
2 tbsp (16 g) sesame seeds
1 tsp dried oregano
1 tsp dried basil
Maldon salt flakes

Preheat the oven to 390°F (200°C). Line two baking sheets with parchment paper.

In a bowl, whisk together the flour, thyme and salt.

In another bowl, combine the tomato purée and water.

Mix the tomato purée and water mixture and olive oil into the dry ingredients. Knead everything gently into a dough. Do not overwork the dough.

Divide the dough into thirds and roll each third into about a ¼-inch (6-mm)-thick dough.

Make the cookies with a 2-inch (5-cm) cookie cutter and place them close to each other on the parchment paper. The cookies do not spread.

In a bowl, mix together the sesame seeds, dried oregano and dried basil. Sprinkle the mixture on top of each cookie and press gently until it sticks. Sprinkle a few flakes of salt on top of each cookie.

Bake the cookies in the oven for about 6 to 8 minutes, or until the cookies are crispy. The baking time depends on how thin the cookies are.

Let the cookies cool on the baking sheet for 10 minutes before moving them onto a cooling rack.

Store the cookies in an airtight container at room temperature for up to 12 days.

# Scrumptious No-Bake Cookies and Bars

I began my vegan baking experiments in 2014 with no-bake cookies and bars. They were the easiest and quickest sweet treats to make, and I was thrilled that something so simple and wholesome as dates and nuts could turn into a delicious crust or cookie.

Some of my favorite sweeteners are featured in this chapter: dates and other dried fruit and maple syrup. Also, a lot of nut butters and tahini are present in this delicious chapter, not only because of their great flavor but also because they bind ingredients together well and provide good fats for the treats.

No-bake cookies and bars are easy to make gluten-free. I use certified gluten-free rolled oats, buckwheat groats, nuts and seeds to make these treats; no flours are needed. I have also snuck in a legume or two because they provide a lovely fudgy texture to treats.

No-bake cookies can be very wholesome, such as the Peanut Butter and Jelly Sandwich Cookies (page 129) with chickpeas and almond flour to add protein to the cookies. Or they can be very indulgent and sweet like the Chocolate Coconut Caramel Cookie Bars (page 141) with gooey coconut caramel, the Caramel Popcorn Cookie Bars (page 137) or the "Snickers" Bars (page 145) with decadent caramel and chocolate layers.

If you want to make a healthier version of traditional Oreos or carrot cake, I have the recipes for you! Or if you want a wholesome treat with lots of nuts and seeds, choose the Date Crunch Bar (page 134) instead.

I hope you enjoy these delicious no-bake treats, which are yummy either as a sweet snack or dessert!

# Peanut Butter and Jelly Sandwich Cookies

Protein rich, gluten-free no-bake cookies that taste like peanut butter and jelly sandwiches are a great snack or a healthier treat to indulge in. Unlike the original PB & J version, these satisfying cookies contain fresh raspberries instead of jam. When you are craving a sweeter treat, just use raspberry jam.

Like many no-bake cookies, these wholesome sandwich cookies require minimal effort: blend, roll, flatten and refrigerate. There is one extra step though, which I really recommend: coat the cookies in sugar to get a sweet crunch with every bite!

## Yield: 10 sandwich cookies

⅓ cup (60 g) cooked chickpeas

¼ cup (60 g) peanut butter

¼ cup (60 ml) maple syrup

1½ cups (150 g) blanched almond flour (see Tips)

¼ cup (25 g) gluten-free oat flour

1 tsp vanilla extract

¼ tsp salt

2 tbsp (30 g) granulated sugar to coat cookies

10–20 fresh raspberries, depending on the size of the berries

In a blender or food processor, blend the cooked chickpeas, peanut butter and maple syrup until smooth, about 2 to 3 minutes. In a bowl, mix together the flours, vanilla extract and salt. With a spoon, combine the dry and wet ingredients until you have a thick, solid cookie dough.

Take 1 tablespoon (15 g) of the dough and roll it into a small ball (you should make 20 balls). Coat each ball in sugar and flatten each into a cookie about ½ inch (1 cm) thick and 1½ inches (4 cm) in diameter.

Place one or two raspberries on each cookie and press another cookie on top. Squeeze the raspberry to flatten the cookie sandwich.

Let the cookies set in the fridge for 30 to 60 minutes.

Store the cookies in the refrigerator for up to 4 days.

*Tips:* You can also store the sugar-coated cookies without raspberries in the freezer. Remove from the freezer about 30 minutes before serving, and when they are softer squeeze a raspberry between two cookies right before eating.

You can make your own blanched almond flour: Just blend blanched almonds in a high-speed blender or food processor until you have a coarse flour, about 3 minutes.

# Carrot Cheesecake Cookies

Carrot cake is one of my favorite cakes, but sometimes a cake is just too much, too sweet or too... cakey. That's when these delicious gluten-free Carrot Cheesecake Cookies come into play! They are beautifully flavored with carrot cake spices such as cinnamon and sweetened with dried apricots, a delicious fruity flavor match with carrots. The filling is a soft vegan cream cheese mixed with confectioners' sugar and lemon juice for a citrusy tang.

### Yield: 16 sandwich cookies

1 cup (90 g) gluten-free rolled oats

½ cup (70 g) cashews

½ cup (55 g) finely shredded carrots

½ cup (90 g) dried apricots

2 tbsp (30 ml) maple syrup

1 tbsp (14 g) coconut oil, room temperature and scoopable

2 tsp (5 g) cinnamon

¼ tsp nutmeg

¼ tsp cloves

¼ tsp salt

### Cream Cheese Filling

⅓ cup (80 g) gluten-free vegan cream cheese, room temperature

¼ cup (30 g) confectioners' sugar

1 tbsp (15 ml) coconut oil, melted

½ tbsp (7.5 ml) lemon juice

Zest of 1 lemon

Pinch of salt

In a blender or food processor, blend together the rolled oats, cashews, shredded carrots, dried apricots, maple syrup, coconut oil, cinnamon, nutmeg, cloves and salt. Roll the cookie dough on parchment paper until it is about ⅕ inch (5 mm) thick.

Make the cookies with a 2-inch (5-cm) round cookie cutter.

To make the filling, in a blender or food processor, mix together the vegan cream cheese, confectioners' sugar, melted coconut oil, lemon juice, lemon zest and salt. If the filling is too liquid, store it in the freezer for 15 minutes. Spread about 1 teaspoon of filling on a cookie and press another cookie on top.

Let the cookies set in the refrigerator for about 30 minutes.

Store the cookies in the refrigerator in an airtight container for up to 4 days, or in the freezer for up to 1 month.

# Rainbow "Oreos"

One of the first vegan cookies I made was a no-bake version of the classic Oreo cookie. My version is a wholesome almond-buckwheat cookie with a fun and tasty crunchy texture. The cookie is filled with a smooth coconut butter and confectioners' sugar mixture colored naturally with turmeric, berry and spirulina powders for beautiful bright and pastel colors.

## Yield: 18 "Oreos"

½ cup (75 g) almonds
⅓ cup (60 g) buckwheat groats
3 tbsp (16 g) cocoa powder
⅛ tsp salt
3 tbsp (45 g) almond butter
2 tbsp (27 g) coconut oil, room temperature and scoopable
4 tbsp (60 ml) maple syrup

### Filling
⅓ cup (80 ml) coconut butter, melted
½ cup (60 g) confectioners' sugar
¼ tsp berry powder
⅛–¼ tsp turmeric powder
⅛ tsp spirulina powder

In a blender or food processor, blend the almonds, buckwheat groats, cocoa powder and salt until you have a coarse flour, for about 2 minutes.

Add the almond butter, coconut oil and maple syrup and keep blending until you have a cookie dough, about 1 to 2 minutes.

If the cookie dough feels too warm to handle, chill it in the refrigerator for 15 minutes.

Roll the cookie dough about ⅕ inch (5 mm) thick. Make cookies with a 2-inch (5-cm) round cookie cutter.

To make the filling, in a bowl, mix together the melted coconut butter and confectioners' sugar with a spoon. Divide the mixture into three bowls and color each mixture with the different powders: the berry powder, turmeric powder and spirulina powder.

Spread the filling on a cookie and press another cookie on top.

Store the cookies in an airtight container in the refrigerator for up to 5 days, or in the freezer for up to 2 months.

# Date Crunch Bars

This is a snack bar at its simplest: dates, nuts, seeds and some quinoa pops or Rice Krispies to get the perfect crunch. This snack is very easy to make, and my children love to make it too. You don't need a food processor to make this, just mix soaked dates, nuts, seeds and pops or Krispies in a bowl and press it into the bottom of a loaf pan. Adjust the sweetness level by choosing either sweet vegan milk chocolate or vegan dark chocolate. We usually opt for 80% dark chocolate, which still tastes pretty sweet with the dates. This bar is naturally gluten-free when gluten-free quinoa pops or Rice Krispies are used.

### Yield: 10 bars

1 cup (200 g) pitted dates such as medjool dates

⅓ cup (50 g) chopped almonds

⅓ cup (50 g) pumpkin seeds

⅓ cup (50 g) sunflower seeds

⅓ cup (20 g) quinoa pops or gluten-free Rice Krispies

¼ tsp salt

¾ cup (130 g) vegan dark chocolate

1½ tsp (7 g) coconut oil, room temperature and scoopable

Line the bottom of a loaf pan with parchment paper.

Soak the dates in a bowl covered with warm water for about 10 minutes to make them tender.

Toast the chopped almonds, pumpkin seeds and sunflower seeds in a dry pan over high heat for a minute or two. Let them cool on a plate for a few minutes.

Drain, dry and chop the dates into tiny pieces. Soften the dates with your hands to a gooey consistency.

In a bowl, mix together the toasted almonds, seeds, quinoa pops, chopped dates and salt. Work the mixture thoroughly with your hands to make the dough sticky. Press the dough into the loaf pan.

Melt the chocolate and coconut oil on the stovetop by first filling a saucepan with about 1 inch (2.5 cm) of water. Place the chocolate and coconut oil in a heatproof bowl on top of the saucepan. Make sure the bowl is not touching the water and that no water gets in the chocolate bowl (or else the chocolate will become lumpy). Warm the chocolate on medium heat, stirring for about 2 minutes, or until the chocolate is smooth. Pour the chocolate on top of the date and nut mixture in the loaf pan.

Let it cool in the refrigerator for about 30 minutes or an hour. Cut the snack into bars with a hot sharp knife.

Store the bars in an airtight container in the refrigerator for up to 8 days, or in the freezer for up to 3 months.

*Tip:* Dip the knife in hot water and wipe the knife dry before cutting each bar.

# Caramel Popcorn Cookie Bars

Pop some popcorn and make a fun treat! These gluten-free Caramel Popcorn Cookie Bars are made from four main ingredients, with popcorn and dates as the main components and nut butter and coconut oil to make it all stick together. Coat the bars in a lush caramel layer and dip them in melted vegan milk chocolate for the ultimate sweet and salty treat!

## Yield: 8 large or 16 small bars

2 cups (20 g) air-popped popcorn

½ cup (100 g) pitted medjool dates

¼ cup (60 g) almond butter or cashew butter

2 tbsp (27 g) coconut oil, room temperature and scoopable

¼ tsp salt

Caramel

⅓ cup (80 g) almond butter

¼ cup (60 ml) maple syrup

1–3 tbsp (15–45 ml) plant-based milk such as oat milk

Pinch of salt

½ cup (85 g) vegan milk chocolate

*Tip*: When blending the popcorn into flour, make sure there are no hard corn kernel parts left. If you see some, just pick them out before mixing the dough.

Line an 8 x 8-inch (20 x 20-cm) pan with parchment paper.

In a blender or food processor, blend the popcorn until it resembles a very coarse flour.

Blend the popcorn, pitted dates, nut butter, coconut oil and salt together.

The dough should be easy to shape and not too crumbly. If it feels too crumbly, add 1 date at a time and blend.

Press the dough into the prepared pan.

To make the caramel, in a bowl, mix together the almond butter, maple syrup, plant-based milk and salt until you have a smooth caramel. Adjust the amount of plant-based milk to reach a gooey caramel consistency.

Spread the caramel layer on top of the cookie bar and freeze it for 60 minutes. Cut it into bars.

Melt the vegan milk chocolate on the stovetop by first filling a saucepan with about 1 inch (2.5 cm) of water. Place the chopped chocolate in a heatproof bowl on top of the saucepan. Make sure the bowl is not touching the water and that no water gets in the chocolate bowl (or else the chocolate will become lumpy). Warm the chocolate on medium heat, stirring for about 2 minutes, or until the chocolate is smooth. Dip the cold caramel popcorn cookie bars in warm milk chocolate. You can also drizzle the chocolate on top of the cookie bars.

Store the cookies in the freezer for up to 3 months.

# Peppermint Rice Krispies Bars

If you need a yummy, crunchy sweet treat for the holidays or any time of year, this is what I recommend: a crushed peppermint candy-filled Rice Krispies bar! This fun treat is loved by both children and adults. It is easy to make with a delicious date and cashew butter base and crushed peppermint candy and Rice Krispies as the main ingredients. Try this with melted vegan white chocolate stripes for an even sweeter treat. Remember to use gluten-free Rice Krispies if you want to make this treat gluten-free.

## Yield: 16 bars

1 cup (200 g) pitted medjool dates

⅓ cup (80 g) cashew butter

3 tbsp (40 g) coconut oil, room temperature and scoopable

3 tbsp (15 g) cocoa powder

¼ tsp salt

½ cup (80 g) crushed peppermint candy canes, plus more for topping

3 cups (90 g) Rice Krispies

¼ cup (40 g) vegan white chocolate

1 tsp coconut oil, room temperature and scoopable

Line an 8 x 8-inch (20 x 20-cm) pan with parchment paper.

If the dates are very hard, soak them in warm water for 15 minutes. Squeeze out the water and pat them dry.

In a food processor or blender, blend the dates, cashew butter, coconut oil, cocoa powder and salt into a smooth paste.

In a bowl, mix together the date paste with the crushed peppermint candy canes and Rice Krispies.

Press the dough into the prepared pan and freeze it for 1 hour.

Melt the vegan white chocolate and coconut oil on the stovetop by first filling a saucepan with about 1 inch (2.5 cm) of water. Place the chocolate and coconut oil in a heatproof bowl on top of the saucepan. Make sure the bowl is not touching the water and that no water gets in the chocolate bowl (or else the chocolate will become lumpy). Warm the chocolate on medium heat, stirring for about 2 minutes, or until the chocolate is smooth. With a spoon, drizzle the white chocolate as stripes on top of the treat. Sprinkle crushed peppermint candy on top.

Cut the Rice Krispies treat into bars or squares.

Store them in the refrigerator in an airtight container for up to 5 days, or in the freezer for up to 3 months.

# Chocolate Coconut Caramel Cookie Bars

This is what happens when a Bounty bar and a Mars bar meet: Chocolate Coconut Caramel Cookie Bars! A thick layer of date caramel on a coconutty crust dipped in lush vegan chocolate. Coconut butter is the ingredient making these delicious bars taste creamy and rich. Did you know you can make coconut butter by blending shredded coconut in your high-speed blender or food processor? Add 1 or 2 teaspoons of coconut oil to make it blend better. Keep on blending until you have a smooth buttery consistency. Use gluten-free rolled oats to make these caramel bars gluten-free.

### Yield: 10 bars

**Crust**
1 cup (90 g) gluten-free rolled oats

¾ cup (70 g) + 1 tbsp (6 g) shredded coconut, divided

¼ cup (55 g) coconut butter

4 tbsp (60 ml) maple syrup

¼ tsp salt

**Caramel Layer**
¼ cup (55 g) coconut butter

1 cup (200 g) pitted soft dates

3 tbsp (45 ml) plant-based milk such as oat milk, room temperature or warmed

⅛ tsp salt

**Chocolate Layer**
1 cup (170 g) vegan chocolate chips or chunks

2 tsp (9 g) coconut oil, room temperature and scoopable

**Tip:** You can also make these bars thicker by using a smaller, rectangular pan such as an 8 x 4-inch (20 x 10-cm) pan.

Line an 8 x 8-inch (20 x 20-cm) pan with parchment paper.

To make the crust, in a food processor or blender, blend the rolled oats and ¾ cup (70 g) of the shredded coconut until you get a coarse flour, about 2 to 3 minutes. Melt the coconut butter and add it with the maple syrup and salt to the flour. Blend everything together until a dough forms. Press the dough into the parchment paper–covered pan.

To make the caramel layer, melt the coconut butter in a bowl in the microwave for about 20 seconds. In a food processor or blender, blend the pitted soft dates, coconut butter, plant-based milk and salt until you have a smooth caramel.

Spread the caramel on top of the crust and store it in the freezer for at least 30 minutes.

To make the chocolate layer, melt the chocolate and coconut oil on the stovetop by first filling a saucepan with about 1 inch (2.5 cm) of water. Place the chocolate and coconut oil in a heatproof bowl on top of the saucepan. Make sure the bowl is not touching the water and that no water gets in the chocolate bowl (or else the chocolate will become lumpy). Warm the chocolate on medium heat, stirring for about 2 minutes, or until the chocolate is smooth.

Cut the solid caramel bars into pieces and dip them into the melted chocolate. Roll the bar around to coat it evenly on each side. Place the bar on a rack and repeat the process until you have coated all the bars with chocolate. Sprinkle the remaining tablespoon (6 g) of shredded coconut on top of each bar.

Store the chocolate bars in the freezer for up to 2 months and take them out about 15 minutes before serving, or eat right away when cold.

# Fudgy Tahini Cookie Dough Bars

These delicious Fudgy Tahini Cookie Dough Bars come with a surprisingly wholesome ingredient: chickpeas. Together with the smooth tahini and coconut butter, chickpeas give these cookie dough bars a delightfully rich texture and fudginess. These bars are sweetened with both dates and maple syrup to make them taste like dessert, and they are gluten-free.

## Yield: 14 bars

1 cup (90 g) gluten-free rolled oats

¼ cup (40 g) cooked chickpeas

½ cup (100 g) pitted dates such as medjool dates

¼ cup (60 ml) maple syrup

¼ cup (60 g) smooth tahini, hulled seed

¼ cup (60 ml) melted coconut butter

¼ tsp salt

⅓ cup (55 g) chocolate chips

Prepare an 8 x 4-inch (20 x 10-cm) dish by lining it with parchment paper. I use a freezer-friendly silicone mold.

In a blender or food processor, blend the rolled oats until you have a smooth flour, about 2 to 3 minutes. Add in the cooked chickpeas, pitted dates, maple syrup, tahini, melted coconut butter and salt. Blend until everything is smooth, about 2 minutes.

Fold in the chocolate chips and press the dough into the mold. Use wet hands if the cookie dough is too sticky.

Freeze the dough for 45 minutes before cutting it into squares or bars.

Store it in the freezer for up to 3 months.

# "Snickers" Bars

These bars taste like Snickers bars, but they are even better knowing the ingredient list is short and wholesome. These sweet and salty bars are fun and quick to make. You can adjust the level of sweetness by using sweet vegan milk chocolate or a darker vegan chocolate as the top layer. If you need more convincing to make these, think of a thick gooey peanut butter caramel layer, crunchy salted peanuts and velvety chocolate on top—that's what "Snickers" is all about, and it's easy to create this popular treat at home!

## Yield: 12 bars

### Crust
1 cup (90 g) rolled oats

⅓ cup (50 g) almonds

¼ cup (60 g) almond butter

4 tbsp (60 ml) maple syrup

2 tbsp (27 g) coconut oil, room temperature and scoopable

¼ tsp salt

½ tsp vanilla extract

### Caramel Layer
⅔ cup (170 g) smooth peanut butter

3 tbsp (45 ml) maple syrup

1½ tsp (8 ml) coconut oil, melted

Pinch of salt

### Nut Layer
½ cup (75 g) salted roasted peanuts, whole

1 tbsp (15 ml) maple syrup

### Chocolate Layer
¾ cup (125 g) chocolate chips or pieces of chocolate

1½ tsp (7 g) coconut oil, room temperature and scoopable

Line a freezer-friendly 8 x 8-inch (20 x 20-cm) pan with parchment paper.

In a food processor or blender, blend the rolled oats and almonds into a coarse flour for about 2 minutes. Add the almond butter, maple syrup, coconut oil, salt and vanilla extract and keep blending until you have a solid dough.

Press the dough into the prepared pan and set it aside.

In a bowl, mix together the smooth peanut butter, maple syrup, melted coconut oil and salt until everything is well combined. Spread the caramel layer on top of the dough.

In a bowl, mix the salted roasted peanuts with the maple syrup and spread the mixture evenly on top of the caramel.

Melt the chocolate and coconut oil on the stovetop by first filling a saucepan with about 1 inch (2.5 cm) of water. Place the chocolate and coconut oil in a heatproof bowl on top of the saucepan. Make sure the bowl is not touching the water and that no water gets in the chocolate bowl (or else the chocolate will become lumpy). Warm the chocolate on medium heat, stirring for about 2 minutes, or until the chocolate is smooth. Spread the melted chocolate layer on top of the peanuts.

Let the "Snickers" firm up in the freezer for at least 30 minutes. Cut it into bars.

Store the bars in the freezer for up to 2 months.

# Notella Cookie Bars

This is a Notella Cookie Bar treat with a secret wholesome ingredient that you will never taste. This ingredient is avocado! It gives the bars a creamy texture together with the aromatic hazelnut butter. Hazelnut butter, cocoa powder and a little sweetener are enough to achieve the perfect Nutella flavor. This treat surely is a much healthier and richer version of the traditional Nutella, and in my opinion a much tastier version too!

## Yield: 9 big bars or 18 smaller bars

¾ cup (70 g) gluten-free rolled oats

¾ cup (90 g) hazelnuts

½ cup (100 g) pitted dates such as medjool dates

⅓ cup (80 g) avocado

¼ cup (25 g) cocoa powder

2 tbsp (27 g) coconut oil, room temperature and scoopable

¼ tsp salt

### Frosting
¼ cup (60 g) hazelnut butter

1 tbsp (5 g) cocoa powder

¼ cup (60 ml) maple syrup

1 tbsp (14 g) coconut oil, room temperature and scoopable

¼ cup (30 g) toasted chopped hazelnuts

Prepare a small 8 x 4-inch (20 x 10-cm) dish by lining it with parchment paper. I use a freezer-friendly silicone mold.

In a food processor or blender, blend the rolled oats and hazelnuts until you have a coarse flour, about 2 minutes.

Add the pitted dates, avocado, cocoa powder, coconut oil and salt and keep blending for about 2 minutes until everything is combined into a dough.

Press the dough into the prepared dish.

To make the frosting, in a bowl, mix together the hazelnut butter, cocoa powder, maple syrup and coconut oil with a spoon. Spread the frosting on top of the cookie dough. Sprinkle the toasted chopped hazelnuts evenly on top.

Freeze it for 30 minutes and cut it into bars or squares.

Store the bars or squares in the freezer for up to 2 months.

# Acknowledgments

First and foremost, *thank you* for holding this book in your hands, for reading the words I am writing on the last day of the year 2020. I am so grateful for your support! I am thankful for you reading my blog, visiting my Instagram, making my recipes and leaving kind comments. You are the reason I wanted to create this book. I love you all, and I'm sending you a big warm hug.

Thank you to the best and most patient family for your support. Thank you for tasting a zillion cookies and giving me honest feedback; thank you for letting me cry and laugh and just be the crazy me that I am when I'm working on a passion project. To Kai, Julia, Lasse, Linda, mom and dad, Laura, Hannes, Leon, Emil and Honey: Thank you for your love and thank you for believing in me! I love you!

Thank you to my friends for your friendship, kind encouragement and support during these years as a food blogger and entrepreneur. Your support and love mean the world to me. Thank you, Tiina, Laura, Paula and Anna, for being here!

I have connected with a community of fellow food bloggers and creators on Instagram, and these connections have formed into virtual and very real friendships. I love you, and I am forever grateful for your continuous support through the years. Thank you, Alex (chocolateandavocados), Belinda (bel.licious), Bianca (thegreencreator), Corey (thevegansix), Dee (greensmoothiegourmet), Haley (sageandfable), Helen (astepfullofyou), Jacky (plantastybites), Maja (delicious_and_healthy_by_maya), Margarida (daisyandthyme), Meera (thefitfabfoodie), Michelle (michelle.nicole.gerrard), Mitra (nutriholist), Natalie (feastingonfruit), Nora (javanese_vegan), Rebecca (thezestylime), Robin (robinwerner.nutrition), Samantha (samanthahadadi), Sara (sarapantovic_), Sarah (sculptedkitchen) and Susanna (eatsleepgreen).

A big thank you to Page Street Publishing and a virtual hug to Madeline Greenhalgh for sending me the most positively surprising email in the hot month of July 2020. Thank you for an inspiring virtual meeting where we brainstormed cookbook ideas, and thank you Madeline and Will for coming up with this fantastic idea about a vegan cookie book! I felt in my heart from the very start that this subject was made for me; I am passionate about vegan baking and especially about cookies! In July when I started working on this secret cookbook project, I felt like something inside me awoke, and now I know what it was: it's the eleven-year-old Tiina who loved to bake chocolate chip cookies.

So there is also one more person I need to thank: I want to say thank you to myself, and especially to my younger self, for developing a passion for cookie baking together with my best friend. We created a cooking and baking club at the tender age of twelve. I think we mostly did it because we had a great excuse to bake sweet treats every day.

I'm also thanking my older self, the Tiina I am now, a hard-working, creative and extremely passionate vegan baker who, with the help of many loving people, created *Fantastic Vegan Cookies*, a book I am very proud of.

# About the Author

Tiina Strandberg is a mom of three living in southern Finland. She is a recipe and content creator, cookbook author and holistic health coach with a focus on plant-based foods. Tiina started the My Berry Forest Instagram and blog in 2015 to share family-friendly vegan recipes approved by her picky children.

Tiina is a self-taught vegan chef and baker. She has been cooking and baking vegan since 2014. She learned to cook and bake by watching her gourmet home-chef parents conjure up the most delicious meals and treats throughout her childhood and youth. Her parents, with their expertise in cooking and baking, are a vital part of the My Berry Forest team.

In her cooking and baking, Tiina focuses on seasonal and creative plant-based ingredients. She is most passionate about vegan baking and the possibilities of veganizing both classic and trendy recipes and of creating new and unique ones. Her favorite treat to bake is cookies.

The biggest inspiration for her vegan creations comes from the beautiful Nordic nature and its changing seasons. One of her favorite pastimes besides baking is taking therapeutic walks in the nearby forests.

Tiina's work has been featured on the cover and pages of *Thrive* magazine, *VegNews* magazine, feedfeed and Best of Vegan as well as recipe features on Well + Good, Tasty and BuzzFeed.

Instagram: @myberryforest

www.myberryforest.com

# Index